DRUG
COURIERS
A New
Perspective

THE **Howard League Handbooks**

Volume I
Perspectives on Violence
edited by Elizabeth A. Stanko

Volume II
Drug Couriers: A New Perspective
edited by Penny Green

Volume III
Policing Matters: Policing Changes
edited by Dick Hobbs

DRUG COURIERS

A New Perspective

edited by Penny Green

Quartet Books

100&852799

First published by Quartet Books Limited 1996
A member of the Namara Group
27 Goodge Street
London W1P 1FD

Copyright © The contributors and the Howard League 1996

The article by Dennis Walton is the property of the Crown. (see page 190.)

A catalogue record for this title is available from the British Library

ISBN 0 7043 7103 0

Phototypeset by Intype London Ltd
Printed and bound in Great Britain

Table of Contents

Preface *Frances Crook*   vii

Introduction *Penny Green*   xiii

I Analyses of Trafficking and Traffickers

1. Drug Couriers: The Construction of a Public Enemy   3
   Penny Green

2. Nigeria, Drug Trafficking and Structural Adjustment   21
   Laurie Joshua

3. Discourses, Perceptions and Policies   30
   Rosa del Olmo

4. Prisoners of War: Women Drug Couriers in the United   46
   States
   Tracy Huling

5. Drug Couriers: The Response of the German Criminal   61
   Justice System
   Hans-Jörg Albrecht

II Practitioner Analysis and Research

1. The Sentencing of Drug Couriers   79
   Rudi Fortson

2. Deportation and Drug Couriers   112
   Alison Stanley

3. A Prison Within a Prison – 4 Years On   127
   John Hedge and Ayesha Tarzi

4. Working with Foreign Offenders: A Role for the   136
   Probation Service
   Rosemary Abernethy and Nick Hammond

5. Turning Back the Clock: the Implications of the   151
   Criminal Justice and Public Order Act 1994 for Pre-
   Sentence Reports
   Nick Hammond

6. Hibiscus: Working with Nigerian Women Prisoners   160
   Olga Heaven

III Perspectives on Law Enforcement

1. Drug Markets and Law Enforcement in Europe   169
   Nicholas Dorn

2. Drug Couriers: The Role of Customs and Excise   183
   Dennis Walton

3. The Policing of Drugs in London   191
   John O'Connor

Acknowledgments   199

About the Contributors   200

Preface

The Howard League was established in 1866, the year that the first Royal Commission on Capital Punishment brought out its report which abolished public executions. Leading philanthropists decided to set up an organization which would work for prison and penal reform as well as continue to press for abolition of the death penalty. It was called the Howard Association, after John Howard who had been the first prison reformer. In 1921 this organization merged with the Penal Reform League to become the Howard League for Penal Reform.

The Howard League cherishes its independence. It has never accepted any government funding and relies entirely on voluntary contributions from individuals and trusts and income from subscriptions and events.

The core of the work involves investigating and commenting on penal policy and practice. The Howard League commissions original research on the penal system which is published in report or book form. The Howard League also publishes occasional papers and briefings as well as factsheets which are regularly up-dated. Since the 1920s the *Howard Journal of Criminal Justice* has appeared quarterly and provides rigorous academic analysis. There is also a membership magazine which keeps supporters informed of Howard League activities and concerns.

Over the years the Howard League has achieved many changes. It has continued the campaign to abolish capital punishment, led the campaign to abolish corporal punishment and helped establish probation.

The League runs vigorous public education campaigns:

- Children in prison. The Howard League believes that 15-year-old boys and girls are too young to be locked up in prisons. They can be managed effectively in the community using the wide range of schemes available. The Howard League absolutely opposes the new secure training centres for children aged 12, 13 and 14.

- Suicides in prison. The Howard League first raised the issue of people committing suicide in prison. It has conducted research, published reports and factsheets, held conferences and meetings with MPs and kept in contact with the families.

- Over-use of prison. The Howard League believes overcrowding is a symptom of a more profound problem: too many people are sent to prison on remand and under sentence. It is not possible, or desirable, to build our way out of this. We should reduce the use of prison in the first place. The Howard League examined who goes to prison, published factsheets on imprisonment for debt and other trivial offences and raised the issue in Parliament.

- Developing alternatives. Most people can be managed effectively in the community. The Howard League works closely alongside probation, social services, police, magistrates and voluntary agencies to encourage the development of alternatives.

- Prisoners' families. Children and families as a whole have a right to keep in close contact, and this gives prisoners the best chance of resettling. The Howard League produced the first ever guide to visiting prisons for families. It held ten workshops inside prisons to open them up to the community and families, and published a report called 'Families Matter' which generated a great deal of local media coverage. As a result, many prisons are improving their visiting facilities.

Our many activities include:

- Original research on a wide range of issues of public concern: commercial prisons, mothers behind bars, prison conditions, racial discrimination, foreign nationals in prison, are just a few recent subjects. The Howard League also publishes briefings on legislation, and sets up working groups to consider aspects of penal policy and practice.

- Conferences for professionals and anyone interested in the criminal justice system, on issues like young people and crime, race, violence, minorities and European prisons. The Howard League holds a conference at New College, Oxford, every year on a major theme of national concern which lasts three days, and it often organizes one-day or evening events.

- A public information service, for schools, students, the media and MPs. The Howard League publishes factsheets on thirty different topics, a video and teachers' notes on the prison system, booklets and briefings.

- Political briefing. We work closely with politicians by providing factual information and holding fringe meetings at the national conferences. We meet with ministers, MPs and peers and are asked to appear before Parliamentary Select Committees to discuss our concerns.

- The Howard League was one of the first voluntary agencies to be granted consultative status with the United Nations. We participate in international debates and conferences, advising on penal reform worldwide. The Howard League's international committee monitors how the UK conforms to United Nations human rights standards on penal matters.

The UK sends a greater number of people to prison than any other country in Europe, yet our crime rate remains high. It is obvious to the Howard League that the over-use of prison is part of the crime problem, not a solution to it.

Prison numbers
Each year 23,000 people are sent to prison for not paying a fine.

In 1995 the prison population stood at 52,000, having risen 30% in 3 years. During the 1980s the prison population had always been high, dropping during 1992 and 1993.

15% of male and 23% of female prisoners describe themselves as black or Asian.

Over 73% of the people sentenced to immediate imprisonment in 1993 were convicted of non-violent offences.

25% of the people in prison are on remand.

58% of the people sent to prison on remand will not get a prison sentence or are found not guilty.

Costs

It costs an average of £442 per week to keep someone in prison. It costs £106,000 to build each new prison place, and £620 million is being spent on building new prisons.

Community sanctions are much cheaper, averaging £24 per week.

Prison does not work

50% of men and 34% of women released from prison are reconvicted of another offence within two years. This rises to more than 70% of youngsters.

Prison conditions

Prison conditions vary. As the number of people being sent to prison rises, there is overcrowding and a strain on buildings and staff. Spending cuts threaten the viability of the probation service in many prisons.

Young people in prison

Each year 20,000 young people aged 17 to 20 are sent to prison on remand. 57% of these young men, and 71% of the young women, will not subsequently get a prison sentence.

Average sentence lengths for young men have increased from 9 months to 12 months in six years, and for young women from 6 months to 13 months.

31 teenagers have committed suicide in prison in the last 5 years.

4,000 young people are sent to prison each year for defaulting on fines.

1,600 boys and girls aged 15 and 16 are sentenced to prison each year.

Prison suicides

387 people have taken their own lives in prisons during the last 10 years. Each year the prison service records over 4,000 incidents of attempted suicide and self-mutilation, about half involving teenagers. Three 15 year-old boys have committed suicide in prisons.

Mothers

About 6,000 women are sent to prison on remand or under sentence each year, and about half of them are mothers. The Howard League estimates that about 6,150 children are forcibly separated from their imprisoned mothers every year.

The Howard League has published a wide range of research papers and reports on these and many other penal issues. This book is part of our continuing responsibility to raise public awareness and discussion around penal issues.

The Howard League hopes that the book will contribute to informed public debate and that readers will get in touch with us should they want to know more about our work and our concerns. As a voluntary agency, the Howard League relies entirely upon the goodwill and support of individuals and organizations. We have a growing list of donors and supporters, and new recruits are welcomed.

The views expressed in these articles are those of the individual authors and do not necessarily reflect policies of the Howard League.

Frances Crook
Director of the Howard League
1996

Introduction

Penny Green

Given the policy and intellectual interest that the subject of drug trafficking elicits, surprisingly little attention has focused on the traffickers themselves. This lack of interest has been convenient for government for it has sustained an emphasis in both the literature and policy on issues relating to the supply and interdiction (ie. the interception of drugs en route). The general silence of those academics working in the field of drugs, with respect to those who carry both the drugs and the ultimate punishment for the offence (see Green 1991), has led to literature which effectively leaves intact the stereotype of the murderous, ruthless drug trafficker which exists in media and state mythology.

My own research and that conducted by Nick Hammond and Rosemary Abernethy, Ayesha Tarzi and John Hedges provides strong evidence for the proposition that by bringing the drug courier to the foreground of drugs research, we are forced to understand drug trafficking differently. When couriers become the subject of analysis rather than simply dark anonymous figures who provide the nefarious backdrop for discussions on drug abuse and policing strategies, then as the articles in this collection illustrate, we are led to reflect on the rupturing inequalities which exist between the developed and underdeveloped world, on the consequences of prohibition in terms of the market and on the general bankruptcy of drug law enforcement strategies.

In terms of demystifying the drug courier, criminal justice practitioners and pressure groups have led the way. The Howard League conference on couriers in 1991, the research on foreign prisoners conducted by the Inner London Probation Service in 1990, the work of Women in Prison, including the establishment of the Hibiscus Club, and the pre-sentence report research and policy initiatives pioneered by Middlesex Area Probation Service in 1992/ 93 have made a very significant impact on the way in which drug couriers are now conceptualized. It is probably too early to say whether or not this will be reflected in sentencing practice, policy development or legal reform but given the traditional response of the judiciary and government to research relating to drugs, there is little room for optimism.

The book is organised around three themes: academic analyses of trafficking and traffickers; practitioner informed developments and a selection of enforcement concerns. It is not designed to assist drug enforcement agencies in their pursuit of the trafficker. On the contrary, the primary aim is to analyse and demystify current representations of the trafficker and, in the process, challenge the criminal justice and judicial sanctions applied against them. It also draws out the political economy of the drugs trade, offering material explanations which link third world poverty to the economic and social misery of Britain's inner cities.

My own paper charts the 'war on drugs' demonization of the drug courier in legislation, legal judgment and criminal justice. Against that powerful demonization, the stories of the couriers, their life circumstances and the injustice of their predicaments come to the fore, effectively shattering the myths which sustain the punitive and prohibitionist thinking surrounding drug trafficking. The evidence forces us to consider the links between third world underdevelopment, the drugs trade and responsibilities of the western 'punishing' countries like Britain. What sense is there in focusing a drugs control strategy around the long term imprisonment of the African or Colombian carriers of drugs when western demand for illegal substances, prohibition and third world underdevelopment ensure a continuation of the drugs trade?

By exploring the structural framework of Nigeria's political economy, Laurie Joshua reveals the virtual inevitability of drug trafficking as a potential source of poverty alleviation in that country. His compelling analyses of World Bank economic strategy on the Nigerian social fabric, the relationship between Nigeria's own internal and external economies and the world economy, and the location of powerful Nigerian interests force fundamental questions relating to legacies of colonialism, the nature of the drugs trade and its true beneficiaries.

The theme of underdevelopment is continued in Rosa del Olmo's paper on the impact of western drugs discourse and US narcotics control policies on the Latin American coca producing countries. She also argues that a major shift in the construction of the 'drug problem' emerged within the US administration during the 1980s and 1990s. Reagan, and following him Bush, made drugs an issue of 'national security' and the central concerns of the drug enforcement enterprise became enshrined in US foreign policy. Rosa del Olmo reports how the massive growth in drugs law enforcement of the 1980s was accompanied by a military programme which fused drug control with the issue of national security, particularly in Latin America. She argues this was reflected politically in the shift in drugs discourse from 'sick consumer' and 'criminal trafficker' to 'victim' and 'victimising countries'. As drugs became a problem of 'national security', counter-insurgency became a legitimate means by which to control the scourge of cocaine. In the 1990s, new policy priorities emerge. Drug trafficking has, del Olmo argues, become characterised by its transnational economic quality and US policy has re-oriented to concentrate on the economic disruption of the trade.

While much has been written on America's war on drugs, and the impact of this war on the inner city ghettos of the U.S., almost no attention has been paid to those incarcerated there for carrying drugs across international borders. Tracy Huling's path-breaking work concentrates on the situation facing women drug couriers imprisoned under the draconian U.S. drug trafficking laws. She highlights the fact the low level drug traffickers in the U.S. are disproportionately female and foreign and that there are gender specific features of drug trafficking which demand that women drug couriers deserve special analytical scrutiny. Highly critical of U.S. drug war strategies, she documents the repressive laws operating in the U.S.; attempts to reform those laws; and the lives of the women most adversely affected by them. It is a powerful piece which cautions strongly against complacency and adds an urgency to the reforms she advocates in the U.S. and to the U.K. reforms initiated by practitioners represented in this volume.

Hans Jörg Albrecht provides a very detailed and fascinating account of the response to drug couriers by the German state. The parallels with Britain are manifest and the article provides a very useful comparative study for those concerned with a wider European dimension. Albrecht points to the links between crime and ethnicity which have emerged in the dominant rhetoric around drug trafficking and drug control and documents the way in which that link has been used to foster right-wing arguments against a liberal immigration policy, especially in relation to asylum seekers. He documents the increasingly punitive approach adopted by the German criminal justice system, its focus on drug users and drug importers and the impact on prison composition and overcrowding. The universality of the German experience is reinforced by the evidence contained elsewhere in this volume.

Part Two provides the experiences, the analyses and the research findings of those criminal justice practitioners and pressure group activists whose own work in the courts and prison system prompted initiatives and concern over the evident plight of drug couriers, particularly foreign national couriers in the UK. The pioneering work in this section has been crucial in the development of a new knowledge base which may now inform academic and criminal justice thinking on drug trafficking policy.

Rudi Fortson has written a seminal article on the sentencing of drug couriers. The literature suffers from a dearth of analysis on the sentencing of drug offenders generally and in this rigorous and scholarly account, Rudi Fortson provides what now must be the definitive study on the sentencing of drug couriers.

In her incisive paper, Alison Stanley draws together the racist nature of British immigration law, the policing of drug trafficking and the Secretary of State's power to deport, to provide an analysis which argues that foreign national drug couriers are in fact punished twice by virtue of their nationality. Stanley documents the deportation procedures and their immediate and longer term effects on the imprisoned courier painting a picture of increased misery and discrimination. It is clear from this paper that the relationship between immigration control and the 'war on drugs' is informed by racism and the desire to control state-defined 'problem populations'.

John Hedge and Ayesha Tarzi report on the Inner London Probation Service's work on foreign offenders and chart the development of reform since the publication of their pioneering study, *A Prison Within a Prison*. Their central focus remains the differential experience of punishment, isolation and personal misery faced by the foreign national prisoner incarcerated thousands of miles from his or her family, friends and culture.

The 'Foreign National Illegal Drug Importer Project' is a pioneering scheme developed by the Middlesex Area Probation Service to prepare pre-sentence reports on foreign nationals in order to challenge the prevailing unfair treatment of this particular group of defendants. Rosemary Abernethy and Nick Hammond provide their detailed research findings on the foreign national couriers arrested at Heathrow Airport between September 1991 and September 1993. This paper provides a fascinating insight into action research and the evolving nature of reform-orientated strategies. Again, this paper gives on-the-ground accounts of the particular suffering of foreign national drug couriers and documents the range of agencies and support groups now involved in attempts to alleviate that suffering.

In a follow up study, Nick Hammond explores the value and impact of pre-sentence reports written on foreign national drug couriers. This evaluative research records the views of judges, lawyers, probation officers, prison staff and sentenced foreign national offenders and argues cogently for the retention of PSRs for this group of offenders.

Olga Heaven raises the very particular problems raised by foreign national women convicted of drug trafficking offences. She writes of children left without a mother for many years; of mothers separated by thousands of miles and prison walls from those children and other dependants; of the powerlessness, poverty and despair which exacerbates the tragedy of the prison experience for women in these circumstances. Heaven then documents how recognition of these particular problems led to the establishment of Hibiscus, the pressure group, designed to assist primarily Nigerian and Jamaican women in U.K. prisons communicate with their families and to provide validated background information for the preparation of pre-sentence reports.

Part 3 offers three accounts and perspectives on law enforcement, practice and analysis. Nicholas Dorn explores the impact of the European Union on drug markets and drug law enforcement. He concludes that rather than create new, less restrictive opportunities for those organizing drug trafficking, the single market may lead to an increase in street-level dealing and have no appreciable impact on major drug trafficking operations. Dorn also argues that the increasingly cooperative strategies pursued by European law enforcement agencies will have the effect of reducing the level of corruption which accompanies monopoly crime control agencies.

The article by Dennis Walton provides a basic account of the role of Customs and Excise in relation to drug couriers, and more significantly, represents the dominant, State perception of the problem. In this collection, Walton's arguments are controversial and unpalatable but they are the dominant and manifest expression of State philosophy and policy in respect of drug trafficking. While academics, students and practitioners will have little problem in locating these arguments in government pronouncements, judicial comment and mass media analysis, the inclusion of this paper serves to illustrate the nature and power of the myths surrounding the trafficker. When read in the light of the other contributions, the ideological nature of dominant drug 'knowledge' is more easily revealed.

The final article is a more reflective personal analysis by a retired commander in the Metropolitan Police. John O'Connor considers the complex nature of the problem being policed, the danger of police corruption that drugs law enforcement inevitably brings and the need for urban regeneration if any drugs control strategy is to make an impact. This paper highlights much of the pessimism that individuals working within enforcement agencies feel, and importantly, cautions on the possible limits of reform, the framework of prohibition and street-crime control brings to the major enforcement agencies.

The aim of this book is to bring together the research and practice findings of those who have been working with drug couriers or researching drug trafficking from perspectives which transcend surface appearances and prejudiced representations. The hope is that this work will help to encourage a more rational, informed and reflective drugs policy which will no longer blindly turn to punitive, bigoted and self defeating strategies.

I

Analyses of
Trafficking and Traffickers

1
Drug Couriers: The Construction of a Public Enemy

Penny Green

Introduction

This paper explores one target of Britain's war on drugs – the drug importer, and argues that s/he has become an exemplary 'enemy', redefined in legal and political rhetoric from the courier to the drugs trafficker. Underpinning this analysis is the central argument that this ideological reconstruction, from courier – poor, foreign, visible and vulnerable, into trafficker – wealthy, powerful, manipulative and dangerous – has the effect of diverting attention from the real causes of the social and economic suffering facing millions in Britain (sometimes manifest in illicit drug addiction). The arrest, conviction and punishment of the drug trafficker, is somehow seen as the embodiment of the state's assault on what, it is argued, has already been defined as a central social problem. This strategy of redirecting blame for social malaise from governments onto powerless individuals characterizes much of modern criminal justice with its positivist underpinnings.

In June 1992, the population under sentence in prison for drug offences (in England and Wales) was 3,500. Forty-five percent of these were sentenced for unlawful importation and a further 40 percent were sentenced for unlawful supply or possession with intent to unlawfully supply.[1]

Imprisoning the targeted few has not led to decreasing drug use or to a decrease in drug-related offences.[2] It is apparent that a real resolution to the conditions which lead to drug addiction is not informing the Government's agenda. But illicit drugs themselves are not the problem. For the state it seems, the problem lies with those who use them and why they use them. As Nils Christie observes, 'in all industrialized societies, the war against drugs has developed into a war which concretely strengthens control by the state over the potentially dangerous classes'.[3] It is therefore argued that the war against drugs is primarily about the reassertion of state control. It is a public reminder of common unity against a common enemy, an enemy which is firmly located outside the boundaries of government social and economic policy.

Sitting in Isleworth Crown Court, which services Heathrow airport, in 1989, I was struck by a number of features which seemed to characterize both the nature of the drug importing defendant and their criminal justice disposal as drug traffickers. Firstly, most traffickers appeared to be foreign nationals. Secondly, they appeared to be motivated primarily by poverty and finally, they demonstrated considerable naiveté about the nature of the drugs they had been found to be carrying. Yet these defendants were typically being sentenced to periods of imprisonment of six years and longer, sentences one might imagine as commensurate with vilification afforded the drug czar. They certainly did not conform to the stereotype used so readily by the judiciary to accompany the handing down of punitive sentences, or to the imagery employed in parliament to ease the passage of harsher and more repressive anti-drugs legislation.

The study on which this paper is based set out to explore the reality behind the stereotype. In essence, the aim was to identify, describe and analyze what I might now describe, as a central focus in the British state's ideological war on drugs.[4]

Historical Background: the Emergence of the Trafficker

The criminalization of drug trafficking is a relatively recent phenomenon, yet the offence now commands the most punitive of all maximum sentences – life imprisonment.

Illegal drug controls in Britain did not emerge in any structured sense until the First World War when Regulation 40B of the Defence of the Realm Act was invoked to control the recreational use of cocaine by British troops. Regulation 40B made it an offence for anyone except the medical professions to possess cocaine. With the 1920 Dangerous Drug Act, we see the Home Office attempting to emulate the American penal approach to drug control by proposing penalties for both addicts and prescribing doctors. The Act made it an offence to import, distribute or possess morphine, heroin and cocaine with maximum penalties of a £200 fine or 6 months imprisonment for a first offence.

There followed little movement in illegal drugs legislation until the Misuse of Drugs Act 1971. This statute represented a clear break from the medico-centric approach to drugs policy which had been favoured in the 1950s and 60s. The Misuse of Drugs Act presented a total commitment to crime control policy and a punitive approach to the treatment of drug offenders:

> The treatment of addicts was barely an issue, criminalization was to be rigorously pursued as the main means of stemming what was now becoming to be more widely considered as a threat of frightening proportions.[5]

The Act distinguished between the possession and trafficking of drugs. Trafficking in Class A drugs now carried a maximum penalty of 14 years imprisonment, while possession of heroin carried a reduced maximum penalty of 7 years. The ideological distinction between the two emerged in debates in the 1960s. As Dorn *et al* point out, drug users were described as typically weak personalities, living in deprived environments, misled by wayward peers or unscrupulous drug pushers.[6] Theirs was a medical/psychological problem requiring treatment or counselling. Drug pushers/dealers/ suppliers on the other hand, occupied a very different ideological terrain, typically described as evil, cold-blooded, ruthless and murderers.

The notion of the trafficker emerges in the 'law and order' informed 1980s. Here, at the same time striking coal miners were being labelled by Prime Minister, Margaret Thatcher as the 'enemy within', drug traffickers were presented as the external threat, posing a danger to society hitherto reserved only for terrorists. The Controlled Drug Penalties Act 1985 raised the maximum sentence for drug trafficking to life imprisonment. The drug trafficker, linked ideologically and punitively with the terrorist, had become a pariah.

Sentencing Trends and Official Justifications

During the 1980s, the number of people sentenced to immediate custody for drug offences in Britain almost trebled – from 1,368 in 1979 to 3,855 in 1989, dropping slightly to 3,400 in 1992. In the same period, the proportion of imprisoned drug offenders sentenced to over 5 years more than trebled from 3 percent to 9.6 percent, remaining steady at 9.4 percent in 1992.[7] More disturbing still, has been the dramatic increase in the proportion of drug importers sentenced to over 5 years – from 6 percent in 1979 to 31.2 percent in 1991, falling slightly to 28.6 percent in 1992.[8]

These trends were underpinned by a succession of increasingly punitive measures taken by both the courts and Parliament. In September 1982, Lord Lane, in the leading case *Aramah*,[9] established guidelines for the harsher sentencing of drug importers. He advised that for the importation of any amount of Class A drug, a sentence should not be less than 4 years; for those trafficking in amounts to the value of £100,000 or more; the sentence should be 7 years or more and for trafficking in amounts to the value of £1 million, sentences should fall between 12 and 14 years.

In October 1983, the then Home Secretary, Leon Britton, effectively increased the length of sentence served by severely restricting the right of parole for drug traffickers sentenced to more than five years. The Controlled Drugs (Penalties) Act 1985 increased the maximum penalty for trafficking in Class A drugs from 14 years to life. During the debate on the Bill, Lord Rodney argued life imprisonment was justified because it would '. . . reflect the revulsion society has for these parasites who trade in human misery'.[10] Baroness Cox described traffickers as 'merchants of death', and '. . .despicable people who exploit and who profit handsomely from the misery of drug addiction'.[11] In the House of Commons, Labour MP Robert Kilroy Silk declared: '. . . they are evil men and women who are making huge commercial profits out of the destruction of young lives'.[12]

In relation to importation, Lord Lane had stated in *Aramah*: 'It is not difficult to understand why in some parts of the world traffickers in heroin in any substantial quantity were sentenced to death and "executed".' In light of the new maximum penalty, he revised the sentencing guidelines from *Aramah* in the case of *Bilinski*.[13] Sentences of 7 years or more, where the street value exceeded £100,000, should be increased to 10 years and upwards, where the value exceeded £1 million, to 14 years and upwards.

In June 1994, Lord Taylor, in *R v Aranguren, Aroyewumi, Bioshogun, Littlefield and Gould*, significantly reinforced and strengthened the punitive sentence strategy revised in *Bilinski*. The new case presented an opportunity for the courts to reassess the sentencing of drug couriers but rather than recognizing the case for leniency, Lord Taylor introduced revised sentencing yardsticks in which the weight rather than purity of the drug became the central determinant of the sentencing tariff. This was designed to prevent sentences being lowered as a result of increased availability lowering the street value of drugs such as cocaine and heroin. The court made clear its position on drug couriers by arguing that:

Although making large profits from importing prohibited drugs was morally reprehensible, the main mischief to which the prohibitions were directed by Parliament was the widespread pushing of addictive drugs harmful to the community. It could not serve Parliament's purpose if the more drugs and therefore the lower the street price, the lower the level of sentencing.[14]

The courts have made it clear that reform in the punishment of drug couriers will not be initiated by them.

Seizures by Customs and Excise

When the seizures of controlled drugs by Customs and Excise are examined, it becomes clear that the majority of seizures are for relatively small amounts. In 1993, Customs made 391 cocaine seizures. Of these, 33 were under 1 gram; 232 were between 1 gram and 500 grams; 54 were over 500 grams and under 1 kilo; and 48 were over 1 and under 10 kilos. Only 9 seizures over 10 kilos and 2 were over 100 kilos. A similar pattern emerges with heroin seizures. In 1992, Customs also made 165 heroin seizures:

25 were for amounts under 1 gram; 80 for amounts over 1 gram and under 500 grams; 17 for amounts over 500 grams and under 1 kilo; 33 for amounts over 1 kilo and under 10 kilos and only 7 heroin seizures were over 10 kilos.[15]

In 1992, Customs and Excise reviewed their policy in relation to 'frontier' work. Their new strategy 'is now firmly based on protecting society against the threat of drugs and other prohibited items rather than worrying unduly about petty excess quantities of cigarettes and spirits'.[16]

The war on drugs is now the priority of Customs and Excise but it is difficult to determine precisely how this is to operate. According to the Customs Directorate 'it is not the commissioner's policy for operational reasons to discuss their targeting policy in terms of points of entry, profiling techniques or risk assessment'.[17]

What is clear, however, is that individuals from particular destinations are likely to become increasingly vulnerable to stop and search practices at ports and airports. West Africans, in particular, are highlighted in Custom's Annual Report as presenting a continuing problem. Courier 'profiles' are very important in determining the practices of customs officers at ports of entry. As the Custom's 1992 *Drugs Brief* states 'seizures made in the day-to-day work at ports and airports depend much more on local development of risk assessment wystems, supplemented by officers' experience and initiative in choosing the right passengers and freight consignments to check ...'.[18] According to the Brief, 87 percent of all heroin seized in 1989 was the result of acting on 'profiles' or 'cold finds'; the same method yielded 33 percent of all cocaine seized.[19]

The *Drugs Brief* also confirms the emphasis which Customs place on stopping individual passengers rather than freight, although officials would not reveal operational details. The vast majority of Class A drug seizures are made from individual passengers. In 1989, Customs seized 152 kilos of heroin and 114 kilos of cocaine respectively from air passengers while seizing only 4 and 7kgs respectively from air freight. The individual, it seems, is set to remain the primary target of Customs detection operations.

Sentencing

The sentencing of Class A drug importers was until 1994 based on a tariff, determined by the estimated street value of the drugs imported. The centrality of street value in sentencing and its method of calculation raised serious problems which were systematically ignored by the courts and which have not been addressed by the new weight-based tariff. The first of these problems relates to the uniquely wicked status afforded drug trafficking. What is it about this offence which requires a distinct and pseudo-scientific sentencing tariff? The second problem concerns the mens rea of the defendant. It would seem from the interview data that drug importers, in general, are completely ignorant about the purity and the wholesale/retail values of the drugs they import. These issues are irrelevant to their role as couriers. Why is it, then, that the courts use only this factor to determine the punishment of the courier? Why is it that ignorance on the part of the courier in respect of this central issue is explicitly ruled out as a mitigating factor by Lord Lane's leading judgement in *Aramah*? Couriers, it seems, are being held responsible for decisions, circumstances and issues outside their knowledge, experience and control. The final problem, of less theoretical significance but important for its impact on the sentencing process, was the crude, unreliable and unscientific estimation of street value and its uncritical acceptance in court.[20]

According to the Home Office, 59.6 percent of all illegal drug importers/exporters receive sentences of over two years.[21] In my sample of 899 drug couriers, the courier convicted of a drugs importation charge received an average prison sentence of 6.3 years. Three-quarters of the couriers in the sample received sentences of over 4.5 years; only 7.7 percent were sentenced to terms of imprisonment under 2 years. Statistics do not reveal the class or street value of the drugs.

British couriers received average sentences of 6 years, Nigerians 5.7 years, Jamaican/West Indians 6.1 years and Colombians 8.4 years. But the evidence from this and other studies[22] is that sentencing has little to do with nationality independent of the imported drug's street value or weight. It was evident from the interviews that the vast majority of couriers (certainly over 90 percent of foreign nationals) did not expect to receive terms of imprisonment at all. None of the men and women interviewed in the sub-sample appreciated the draconian nature of British drug penalties or the very long sentences that awaited them. Most had been informed by drug suppliers that the worst that could happen would be that the drugs would be confiscated and they would be deported home on the next available flight.

In 1991, 84 women were sentenced to immediate custody for the importation of illicit drugs.[23] On the whole, sentences for women reflect the sentencing pattern for men. Women tend to be sentenced to periods slightly shorter than men of their own nationality. The sentencing of Nigerian women, however, contradicts this trend – they were punished more harshly than Nigerian men – on average receiving sentences 10 months longer. This reversal of the general pattern might tentatively be explained by the courts' apparent impatience with those women who plead not guilty claiming that they have been duped into carrying drugs. Given the small size of the small sample, it is impossible to generalize. However, six of the Nigerian women in the sub-sample were in this category; each of them received sentences over 6 years, with two receiving sentences of 10 and 12 years. The inclusion of these women in the Nigerian female sample may therefore contribute to a potentially inflated average sentence length.

The issue of mitigation was singled out as a particularly great injustice by couriers. Social Inquiry Reports (replaced by Pre-Sentence Reports with the implementation of the Criminal Justice Act 1991 – see Abernethy and Hammond; and Hammond, this volume) were at the time only prepared on defendants who were either British nationals or resident in Britain. Reports were not prepared on foreign nationals which denied 72 percent of the drug importers facing the very long sentences described above the potential mitigation arising from an SIR.

However, the courts appear to ignore all potential mitigation bar a plea of guilty. Providing assistance to Customs and Excise may mitigate sentence but the evidence suggests that both forms operate inconsistently. The fact that a courier is a first time offender, pregnant, accompanied by children, poverty stricken, motivated only by a desperate need to feed or house his/her family may only harden the judiciary in their war against this already exploited community. In the case of *Aramah*, Lord Lane made plain the court's position on mitigation:

> The good character of the courier is of less importance than the good character of the defendant in other cases . . . the large scale operator looks for couriers of good character and for people of a sort which is likely to exercise the sympathy of the court if they are detected and arrested. Consequently one will frequently find students and sick and elderly people are used as couriers for two reasons: first of all they are vulnerable to suggestion and vulnerable to the offer of a quick profit, and secondly it is felt that the courts may be moved to misplaced sympathy in their case. There are few, if any, occasions when anything other than an immediate custodial sentence is proper for this type of importation.[24]

Given the weight and sentiment of Lord Lane's analysis, it is exceedingly unlikely in the prevailing climate that pre-sentence reports would be given serious consideration by a judge in the process of sentencing a courier. Recent research has revealed that judges are willing to entertain considerable discounts of sentence but only in cases where the estimated street value was between £100,000 and one million pounds. For those importers of lesser amounts (ie the majority), there is virtually no flexibility extended and the four year minimum sentence for Class A importation of 'any amount' is rigidly enforced.[25]

However, the case study of 'Imran' (see below) shows that social class can make a difference. Urbane and articulate, he felt his barrister made out an excellent case for mitigation on the basis that he came from a 'very respectable family' – references from Pakistan confirmed this and 'really convinced the judge'. Both he and his barrister expected a 10 year sentence but he received five years. There are many cases in this study of Nigerian heroin importers, pleading guilty to importing ten times less in quantity, who are sentenced to between 5 and 8 years.

The vast majority of foreign national couriers will serve out their full sentence in Britain. While repatriation treaties exist between Britain, the USA and most European countries, there are no such treaties with the countries whose nationals make up the bulk of the imprisoned courier population.[26]

The Drug Trafficking Offences Act 1986 made confiscation powers available to courts. The legislation specifies that the court leaves the confiscation order out of account when determining the appropriate sentence, thus providing a new and additional punishment for those convicted of trafficking drugs.

The Act provides heavy periods of additional imprisonment for failure to pay any amount exceeding £10,000. Since 1987, the number of confiscation orders applied by the courts has increased significantly, from 203 in 1987 to 1,005 in 1991. The emerging pattern, exemplified by the 1991 figures, is interesting. The vast majority of orders applied since 1987 are made for relatively insignificant sums. The 1991 figures on the 1,005 confiscation orders made by the Crown Court for that year reveal that 719 (71.5 percent) were for amounts under £1000, 121 (12 percent) were for amounts between £1000 and £3000 and 86 (8.5 percent) were for amounts between £3000 and £10,000. Thirty-nine orders (3.8 percent) were for amounts between £10,000 and £30,000 with only 16 (1.6 percent) made for amounts in excess of £100,000.[27]

These figures tend to contradict the policy makers' stated intentions that confiscation orders are targeted at those who make immense profits from drug trafficking. Interviews with five self-employed drug smugglers who are in the position of organising drug imports, revealed that they were generally not subject to confiscation orders despite admitting to considerable wealth acquired as a result of trading in drugs. Each had taken precautions to ensure that their assets could not be traced to themselves. The only self-employed drug smuggler in the interview sample to have a confiscation order applied (for the total sum of £160,000) had ensured that most of his assets were tied up in trust funds in the names of his children.

Who are the Traffickers?

The reality of the drug courier sits very uneasily against this punitive political and legislative background.[28]

Using the data available on the sample of almost 900, we find that almost three-quarters (72 percent) of the sample, imprisoned for the illegal importation of drugs, are foreign nationals. Africans accounted for 35 percent of this population, with the largest national category being Nigerian (30 percent of the total). British couriers represent 28 percent of the population with Jamaican/West Indian at 9 percent, Colombian (5.3 percent), Pakistani (5.1 percent) and Dutch (3.3 percent).

Given media attention and Customs' expressed concern over cocaine and its South American suppliers, it is perhaps surprising to note that only 5.3 percent of the total were Colombian nationals. Couriers from other South American countries were insignificant.

The evidence from this research (and from Home Office and Prison Department Statistics[29]) suggests that approximately 80 percent of all imprisoned couriers are men. Earlier estimates had placed the percentage of women considerably higher – virtually all journalistic and pressure group interest in couriers has been on women – assisting a distorted perception. What is significant, however, is that female drug couriers account for approximately 20 percent of the UK female prison population, whilst male couriers account for only 4 percent of the total male prison population.

It is estimated that there were between 320 and 400 women serving sentences and on remand for the importation of drugs in January 1991 of whom 37.1 percent were African (with 29.4 percent of all the women from Nigeria).

Couriers are not particularly young – the average age being 35.7 years, with 67 percent of the sample aged over 30 years. Half the sample were married or cohabiting, 42 percent single and 7 percent widowed, separated or divorced. Marital status, however, does not seem to be a particularly useful determinant of parental responsibility. The interviews reveal that the majority of single couriers were also responsible for children or other dependants.

Almost one third of the sample were unemployed at the time of arrest and another 14 percent [51 percent women and 30 percent men] were employed in the most menial jobs (cleaners, factory hands, agricultural labourers etc.). Almost 30 percent were self-employed as traders or some other form of business enterprise, but if Nigerians are subtracted from the sample this percentage declines markedly. Very few couriers (less than 5 percent) were professionally employed at the time of arrest, although a significant number of Nigerian men had been professionally trained and employed prior to the Nigerian economic crisis of the mid 1980s. Perhaps, surprisingly, only a very small percentage of couriers were employed by airlines, airports, or in the merchant navy – occupations which 'lend' themselves to drug trafficking. Though of course this might very easily be explained by Customs operational policies.

Case Studies

The following testimonies from four imprisoned couriers provide some sense of the experiences and circumstances which led them to carry drugs. The first three stories are representative and characterize the financial and personal anguish too frequently apparent behind the offence. They also serve too as an antidote to the popular stereotype of the drugs trafficker. The fourth case-study is interesting because it illustrates a departure from the norm and is considered separately in the discussion on sentencing above.

Luke is a 29 year old Nigerian with two children, serving a four and a half year sentence for smuggling 200 grams of heroin (street value = £17,000) packed in false bottomed shoes. He was to be paid £2,000 for his role.

'Thousands of skilled people in Nigeria are unemployed. I graduated in 1984 with a degree in marketing, did my compulsory National Youth Service and have been unemployed since 1985. I met my partner in college, she got pregnant and dropped out. Then my father became very ill with a stroke in 1986 and I couldn't even afford to buy any of the drugs prescribed for him. My sister helped but I'm the only son and the bitterness creeps in when you can't take on the responsibilities you should. So I walked the street for 3 years without a job. You are up against the wall. We don't come from a country where you walk into a bank with a good proposal to set up a business unless you come from the ruling elite. I knew the risks involved, I knew the whole world was against it but you get to the stage where you don't care any more. I was looking for money and was introduced by friends to this man who offered a conditional loan, conditional on running drugs. He didn't threaten or force me – he didn't have to, I was against the wall. When you are in such a situation . . . my orientation has never been criminal, I still don't have criminal tendencies.'

Antonio is a 36 year old Colombian, sentenced to 6 years' imprisonment for the importation of 700 grams of cocaine. He left school at 15 and was unemployed at the time of his arrest, although he was trying to sell jewellery he had made himself. Married with four children, he and his family (none of whom were working) were living in poverty with his mother in a village.

'I had many debts to pay off in my village, so I visited family in Bogota and they gave me some gold statues which I was to sell in Venezuela to start me off. I was going to live in Venezuela for a few months to earn enough money to pay off my debts. But in a coffee house in Bogota I started talking to a man about my debt problems and he told me the solution to my problems was carrying drugs to England, that it was easy and the police would give me no trouble. He said that he would pay off all my debts when I got back. I was given $1,000, then I went to an apartment and was told to swallow 55 packets of cocaine. I wasn't worried, I just thought about the money sorting out my debts.'

Janice is a 22 year old Jamaican resident in the United States. She has 2 brothers and 1 sister. She had been living with her mother (who through illness was unable to work) and aunt, and had been unemployed for the 4 years prior to her arrest. Following her arrest she was convicted ans sentenced to 7 years imprisonment for the importation of 1 kilo of cocaine.

'I needed the money. My brother was attacked by a girl in the West Indies – she threw acid in his face causing terrible injury. The legal and medical fees ran into thousands and thousands of dollars and he had no way of raising the money. I knew some dealers so I decided to bring drugs over to England ... I was aware of what I was doing and why I was doing it, so I don't really regret it but I probably would have thought twice if I'd realised the implications.'

Imran is an upper middle-class Pakistani businessman with a law degree. Convicted of the importation of 1200 grams of heroin (with a street value in the region of £120,000) he received a 5 year sentence. Married, with two children, he was living in the Middle

East returning to visit his family in Pakistan once a month. In the mid 1980s, his company suffered severe economic losses and creditors began applying pressure for payment.

'Up to today I have never even seen drugs and only in the greatest hardship did I take a bad decision – it was the easiest and the quickest way. The local Dubai bank was pressing me. If I paid the bank around $4,000 they would have let me run another year. So, at the same time, I started a building maintenance company and I appointed an engineer who was to get fast money, and put it in the bank to keep my other company going – it wasn't set up as a long term business, but it failed in 2 years. The manager of a company I do business with knew my position and he wanted to help. He said trafficking in drugs was a sure way to make money. There are so many people involved in drugs in Pakistan, it's not difficult to organize.'

The New Europe – there are frontiers and there are *frontiers*

The advent of the single market and the new co-operative law enforcement strategies that are a product of that union are set to further reinforce the policies already in place which target the Third World courier. While the European Union is ostensibly about the relaxation of border controls between member states, those frontiers which are 'exposed' or adjacent to non-European countries are likely to experience increased controls. The work of British Customs and Excise officers will not, for example, be relaxed and will remain organised around drug control. Douglas Hogg, Under Secretary at the Home Office, made clear to the House of Commons in June 1989:

... by treaty and by statute ... we have retained the right to maintain at the ports of entry such controls as we deem necessary to prevent the importation of drugs and other criminal articles.[30]

According to *Statewatch*, a permanent Dutch 'anti-crime' unit has been posted to Paris in order to liaise with French law-enforcers. French border control officers and the Dutch border gendarmerie (*maréchausées*) now reportedly 'work routinely on each other's territory on board international trains', where they check the status of travelling aliens in an attempt to intercept those without a visa while they are still in the country of departure.[31]

As Jenkins rightly foresees, '... in order to compensate for the disappearance of internal frontier controls an exchange of information between police and security authorities is indispensable'.[32] The Trevi Group (and specifically Trevi 30), the Schengen Agreement and the K4 Coordinating Committee have all developed with this purpose in mind.[33]

One of the proposals arising out of the Schengen Treaty is for the development of a comprehensive information scheme and the possibility of pan-European drugs intelligence organization has already been mooted.

But the issue of relaxed border controls is somewhat illusory particularly in respect of the movement of 'non-European' nationals across those borders – an issue pertinent to the drug couriers in my own research study. What appears to have occurred is a melding of drug traffickers with illegal immigrants. European Union is interested in facilitating the movement of only certain kinds of labour – a position suitably reinforced by public representations of drug smuggling illegal 'economic' immigrants. This is exemplified in the statement arising from the Trevi members' Programme of Action, 1990, which expressed their task as a *synthesis of the arrangements ... between police and security services* in relation to *terrorism, drug trafficking or any forms of crime including organised illegal immigration.*[34]

Conclusions

This research provides strong evidence to suggest that drug couriers do not conform to the ungrounded imagery which vilifies them in the public mind. The research profile documents a reality of Third World poverty, of men and women who are generally naive about drugs, of men and women whose offence was not motivated by greed but by familial concerns and financial despair. While there is evidence of a tacit acknowledgement of this reality among customs officials, court officers, politicians and the judiciary, the ideological fusion of the courier with the trafficker stereotype prevails – promulgated by these very authorities.

This fusion serves to ensure the smooth passage of harsh anti-drug legislation, for policing practices targeted at Third World couriers (and black users in the decaying inner cities) and for increasingly punitive prison sentences. The singular emphasis on the nature, street value or weight of the drugs imported and the denial by the courts of mitigation, creates a situation whereby the judiciary absolves itself of any responsibility to address the social and economic circumstances of the courier before them.

Not all drug couriers are naive, not all tell the truth to the academic researcher. Neither issue, however, obscures the central findings of this research. Relative poverty, a sense of desperation, an opportunity to rise above the grinding misery of economic hardship in the developing world, all contribute to a rational explanation of the phenomena.

In reality then, as the evidence from this research illustrates, drug couriers are as far removed from the drugs baron or business entrepreneur who exploits them as they are from the judge who sentences them. Like the baron, politicians, the judiciary and the mass-media also exploit the courier. The drug courier, it would seem, has become an expressive target in the State's offensive against illegal drugs and in the ideological war over who is to blame for drug abuse, the courier provides a cheap, expendable, diversionary scapegoat.

Notes

1. Home Office Statistical Bulletin, 1993, *Statistics of Drug Seizures and Offenders dealt with, UK, 1992.*
2. In fact, according to the Home Office Statistical Bulletin, *Statistics of Drug Addicts Notified to the Home Office, UK, 1993,* the number of newly recorded addicts has continued to rise – between 1990 and 1993 there was a 20% increase, from 6,923 to 11,561.
3. Nils Christie, *Crime Control as Industry: Towards GULAGS Western Style!* (1993) p. 64.
4. *Method*
   The research began as a largely qualitative exercise, locating those prisons which held the highest concentrations of drug importers (information informally obtained through the Probation Service), then interviewing a random sample of couriers in those prisons.

It was rather a case of feeling in the dark. What was known was limited to a specific prison and impressionistic. Official statistics could provide very little about the imprisoned courier – only a figure for the numbers of drug importers imprisoned with no information on nationality, nature and amount of the drug imported or sentence length.

At the time of the research prisons were in the process of introducing computerised records on all inmates. The data available included for each prisoner the main offence, nationality, age, marital status, number of dependents and sentence. Following a request to all prisons in England and Wales data was received from 36 prisons providing basic profile information on almost 900 drug importers (623 male and 276 female). This sample represented approximately half of the estimated 2,000 drug importers serving sentences in British prisons in 1990. A sub-sample of 50 couriers (19 women and 31 men) were selected as representatively as possible given the limitations of prison access and then interviewed in depth.

The interviews were designed to develop a comprehensive profile of the imprisoned courier. The aim was to explore the economic, personal and social circumstances of the drug importer, the factors motivating and surrounding the offence, the nature of the drug transaction and the experience of detention, arrest, conviction and detention.

5. Rutherford, A. and Green, P. 'Illegal Drugs and British Criminal Justice Policy' (1989) in Albrecht, H. J. and Kalmthout, A. (eds) *Drug Policies in Western Europe*, Max Planck Institute: Freiberg p. 387.
6. Dorn, N., South, N. and Murji, K., *Traffickers*, Routledge, London, 1991.
7. Home Office Statistical Bulletin 1990 *Statistics of the Misuse of Drugs: Seizures and offenders dealt with, United Kingdom, 1989* [and *Supplementary Table*], Home Office; Home Office Statistical Bulletin 1993 *Statistics of Drug Seizures and Offenders dealt with, UK, 1992*.
8. Home Office, *Statistics of Drug Seizures and offenders dealt with, United Kingdom, 1991 and 1992 Supplementary tables.* (1992 and 1993).
9. *Aramah* 4 Cr.App.R. (s) 407.
10. Hansard [Lords] Committee stage, Controlled Drugs (penalties) Bill, 27.6.85: 838.
11. Hansard ibid. (27.6.85: 838).
12. ibid.
13. *Bilinski* [(1988) 866. App R 146].
14. *Aranguren, Aroyewumi, Bioshogun, Littlefield and Gould* 1994, 23.s.94 Times Law Reports.
15. (Sources: Table S1.6 H.O. Statistics on the Misuse of Drugs – Supplementary Tables 1992).
16. Customs and Excise, *Drugs Brief*, 1992.
17. Personal communication with J. K. Oxenford, Customs Directorate, 8th March 1991.
18. *Drugs Brief*, op.cit.
19. H.M. Customs and Excise, 1990 *Drugs Brief 1992: Frontier Checks and the Free Movement of People.*
20. See Kay, L. '*Aramah* and the street value of drugs', *Criminal Law Review* 1987, p. 184, for a discussion of the determination of street value. Estimates are based on information gathered by the National Criminal Intelligence Service (NCIS) which in turn are based on local police intelligence and 'police buys' and on laboratory analyses of the purity of a particular drug consignment.

21. Home Office, *Statistics of drug seizures and offenders dealt with*, 1992.
22. See especially P. Green, 1990, *Drug Couriers*, Howard League, London; Green, Mills and Reid, 'The Characteristics and Sentencing of Illegal Drug Importers', *British Journal of Criminology* 1994 forthcoming.
23. See Home Office Research and Statistics Dept. 1992.
24. *Aramah*, ibid.
25. P. Green, C. Mills and T. Reid, 'The Characteristics and Sentencing of Illegal Drug Importers', 1994 *British Journal of Criminology* vol. 34 No. 4 Autumn.
26. For further information on foreign national prisoners see J. Hedges and A. Tarzi, 1990, *A Study of Foreign Prisoners*, Inner London Probation Service; R. Abernethy and N. Hammond et al 1992 *Drug Couriers: a Role for the Probation Service*, Middlesex Probation Service, London.
27. Home Office 1993 *Criminal Statistics England and Wales 1992*, Cm 2410, London: HMSO.
28. Much of this data is drawn from my previously published report *Drug Couriers* 1990, Howard League, London.
29. Home Office 1989, *Prison Statistics in England and Wales*. Cm 1221.
30. Dorn, N. and South, N., 'Drugs, Crime and Law Enforcement: some issues for Europe' in Francis Heidensohn and Martin Farrell (eds) *Crime in Europe*, Routledge, London, 1991.
31. *Statewatch*, May-June 1994, 9.
32. Jenkins, J. 1989 'Foreign Exchange', *New Statesman and Society*, 28 July 1989, 12.
33. See Tony Bunyan, 1994. 'Trevi, Europol and the European State', *Statewatching the new Europe*, Tony Bunyan (ed) Statewatch, London.
34. Cited in Bunyan, *ibid.*, p. 21.

2

Nigeria, Drug Trafficking and Structural Adjustment:
Overcoming the Impediments to Dialogue

Laurie Joshua

Introduction

In her study of drug couriers,[1] Penny Green devoted a substantial part of the research effort to the high proportion of Nigerian couriers in British prisons. This article aims to complement the findings from the study on drug couriers by summarising how the act of drug trafficking commissioned by Nigerian men and women is impelled, in part, by influences that operate within the structural framework of Nigeria's political economy. I attempt to do this by juxtaposing the act of drug trafficking with the impact of the World Bank's economic philosophy on the social fabric of Nigeria, the linkages between Nigeria's domestic and external economies and the global economy, and events which signal the connivance of powerful Nigerian interests on the act of drug trafficking.

The article is underpinned by a thematic argument on overcoming impediments to dialogue on matters of both policy and practice; and highlights the action initiated by Save the Children Fund to construct, influence and inform such dialogue at national and bilateral levels.

The importance of talking and listening is vital to building healthy relationships, and when one occurs without the other the outcome can be embarrassing for both parties. The notion of 'Overcoming the Impediments to Dialogue' is taken from the work of the renowned Nigerian author, Chinua Achebe. In his work published under the title *Hopes and Impediments* (1988), Achebe recounts a scenario in which he was invited to attend a conference in Europe. As a means of ensuring that Mr Achebe received notice of the conference, the organisers sent their invitation through three different emissaries: Nigeria Airways, Radio Nigeria and the Nigeria Police. MrAchebe's reply, as he was to learn upon his arrival in Europe, was never received – a perfect example of one-way traffic and a parable of sorts illustrating my main theme.

Dialogue is central to a full and fair appraisal of the reasons why Nigerian men and women feature so prominently in UK prison populations for the unlawful importation of drugs and demands that three interdependent factors operating within Nigeria's political economy have to be taken into account:

a) the Structural Adjustment Programme (SAP);

b) the degree to which the Nigerian economy, compared with the rest of sub-Saharan Africa is linked to the globay economy; and

c) corruption.

Without taking account of these *three* interdependent factors, we cannot understand the context, and without understanding the context we increase the chances of restricting or mistargeting the frameworks for dialogue.

Structural adjustment

Nigeria has, like many other African countries, been subject to the ravages of a severe programme of economic structural adjustment. The ongoing SAP was set in motion in 1986 under the inspired philosophy of the World Bank, and against a background of declining oil revenues. The philosophy informing this World Bank revolution in Nigeria rested on the premise that national wealth was best increased by allowing free and unrestricted exchange among individuals in both the domestic and international economies. The philosophy essentially argues for limitations on the economic role of government, which the Bank claims intentionally or unintentionally restricts the effective operation of markets and prevents potentially rewarding trades from occurring. The philosophy rests on three central empirical propositions:

a) that individuals are the principal actors within the political economy:

b) that individuals are rational actors – who make cost-benefit calculations across a wide range of options; and

c) that individuals maximise their options by making trade-offs between goods.

It is important to remember that these three empirical propositions are neither true nor false; only useful or useless in advancing arguments of social, political and economic phenomena. It is therefore possible within this frame of reference to argue that some Nigerian men and women, when confronted with adverse domestic economic circumstances, become engaged in the act of drug trafficking on the basis of cost-benefit calculations which seek to maximise their options; and do so by extending the range of goods that are traded within the established pathways that link Nigeria's economy with the global economy. The paradox of this is that for those Nigerian men and women who are arrested, sentenced and imprisoned in the UK, the trade-off actually makes them, and their families, worse off.

Prior to the delivery of the World Bank philosophy and the concomitant umbilical cord of SAP, Nigeria was one of the richest countries in Africa, with an annual income per person of over US$1200 (1985), and was classified by the International Monetary Fund (IMF) as a 'middle income country'. Since the inception of SAP, per capita income has fallen to less than US$250 (1991), and the IMF has reclassified Nigeria as the world's thirteenth poorest nation. This is reflected in some basic social and economic indicators.

Social indicators

Population:	120 million (1990)[2]
Life Expectancy:	Female – 53 years (at birth)
	Male – 49 years (at birth)

Maternal Mortality:	1,500 (per 100,000 live births)
Annual Growth of Population:	3.3 per cent
Infant Mortality:	110 (per thousand live births)

Economic indicators

Gross National Product:	US$29 bn (in 1991), compared with $72 bn (in 1986)
Foreign Debt:	US$33.5 bn (1991)
Foreign Earnings:	US$8 bn (1992 projections)
Foreign Debt Repayments:	60 per cent of Foreign Earnings
Aid Receipts as % of GNP:	0.4 per cent (US$1.00 per head of population)

The impact of this on-going economic revolution has been mixed. The vast majority of urban dwellers, who comprise over 35 per cent of Nigeria's population, have seen their incomes shrink while the cost of living has escalated and the value of the currency – the naira – has depreciated from parity with the £ sterling in 1985 to a value of less than 5 pence in 1992. For rural dwellers, who comprise over 60 per cent of the population, the impact has been more variable – some have seen their real incomes grow. What cannot be denied, however, is that there have been winners and losers, and World Bank figures (1990) show that standards of living in Nigeria are now lower than they were in the 1950s. This level of decline led the World Bank to conclude that for Nigeria 'the economic crisis of the 1980s has been so severe that it has more than cancelled out the progress of the previous twenty years'. More recently, the American Express Bank (1992) recorded that Nigeria's economy, when set against the benchmarks of the Organisation for Economic Cooperation and Development (OECD), suffered the world's worst rate of decline during the 1980s. The socio-economic characteristics of Nigerian men and women in Penny Green's sample, and those in the sample of an earlier report – Prison Within a Prison – compiled by the Inner London Probation Service, denote the profiles of Nigerians whose lives have been most significantly affected by the decline in Nigeria's economic performance.

International Linkage

Nigeria is the world's ninth largest oil producer, holds one-fifth of the world's total supply of natural gas and imports vast quantities of goods and services from other parts of the world. It should therefore not be surprising that Nigeria is one of the European Community's largest trading partners, and that bilateral trade between the UK and Nigeria has, over the last decade, hovered between half a billion and one billion pounds per annum. Given this volume of trade, Nigeria is strategic to, and influenced by, legitimate and illegitimate global interests, and it is not by coincidence that the illegitimate trade of the drug courier should follow the same pathways as those of Nigeria's legitimate trade. The strength of Nigeria's connections to the international global economy is reflected in the fact that Nigeria is served by more international airlines than most other countries in sub-Saharan Africa. This means that flights to Nigeria can be made with relative ease from the drug producing areas in South America, the Middle East and Asia; and from Nigeria to the purchasing areas in Western Europe and North America.

Corruption

The high numbers of Nigerian men and women in British prisons, and the number of children of convicted women accommodated by social services departments, would not be at the current levels without the connivance of 'powerful interests' in Nigeria. The degree to which there is high level involvement in the Nigerian drugs trade can be gleaned from the circumstances surrounding the death of the 'Newswatch' editor, Dele Giwa, who was killed by a parcel bomb in 1986 while investigating the drugs trade; and by the removal of the first Chairman of the Nigerian Drug Law Enforcement Agency in 1991 – on allegations that he was trying, at the behest of others, to free convicted drug traffickers.

The combined effects of the factors outlined above put Nigeria in the unenviable position as a favoured transit point between producers and purchasers. Moreover, the strategic position of Nigeria in the global economy and the continuing deleterious effects of the SAP on the lives of Nigerian families, means that the number of persons from Nigeria, as a proportion of the total number of foreign nationals, arrested, sentenced and imprisoned in the UK for drug importation offences, is unlikely to change significantly. Such an assessment may sound pessimistic but when set against component parts of the next phase of the SAP, including an extending privatisation programme of publicly owned companies and an estimated additional loss of up to 2 million jobs, it has a touch of realism.

Overcoming the impediments to dialogue

Against the background of the factors mentioned above, Save the Children Fund has sought to facilitate and inform debate on Nigerian nationals in prison in the UK, and on the social work arrangements for the children of women who face deportation at the end of their sentence. The Fund set about tackling these tasks through a matrix of policy and practice interventions which aimed to complement the principles of the Children Act 1989, the Criminal Justice Act 1991 and the White Paper 'Custody, Care and Justice'; and by providing forums for the development of dialogue and new initiatives at local, national and international levels.

These initiatives involved:

a) developing and implementing a three-phased Technical Cooperation Training Programmes for Nigerian Government officers. The aim of this is to extend the management and practice capacity of the Nigerian Federal Ministry of Health and Human Services to meet the legal, social and welfare requirements of Nigerian nationals who come into contact with the British criminal justice system. The programme has been funded by the Aid Wing of the Foreign and Commonwealth Office;

b) convening an International Workshop on child care and criminal justice issues in Lagos, Nigeria, in October 1990. The five-day event was attended by 20 social workers and probation officers from the UK, and over 120 delegates from Nigeria. The communiqué issued at the end of the workshop made specific recommendations for action, on a range of issues, by the UK and Nigerian Governments. The workshop and the communiqué formed the foundations for inter-ministerial talks between the Nigerian and UK Governments which took place in January 1991; and for a follow-up visit to the UK by representatives of the Nigerian Government in September 1991;

c) responding to Nigeria's Decree 33 by writing, in October 1990, to Ministers in the Department of Health, the Home Office and the Foreign and Commonwealth office. The objective was to ensure that appropriate social work arrangements were implemented to protect the interests of Nigerian children looked after by local authorities while their mothers are in prison; and whose welfare would be adversely affected by their mothers' further imprisonment in Nigeria. In response to SCF's concerns, the Department of Health issued guidance to all local children whose parent is in custody. The guidance was subsequently amended by, and incorporated into, the Children Act 1989 which came into force in October 1991;

d) convening, during 1990 and 1991, a series of bilateral training seminars on child care and criminal justice issues. These seminars brought together policy makers from UK central government departments, as well as practitioners from the UK and Nigeria. These seminars sought to improve understanding, examine policy and practice issues that impinge upon bilateral child care and criminal justice issues, and to explore strategies that will shape future policies and promote good practice; and

e) working with the Nigeria High Commission in London to extend its capacity to meet the full range of child care and criminal justice issues that affect Nigerian nationals in the UK. The outcome from this collaboration was the appointment of social worker(s) in the High Commission to provide a sustainable source of advice and assistance to UK social work and probation agencies.

As a means of coordinating, managing and monitoring the local, national and international dimensions to these initiatives, SCF set up a policy development group (with 'observers' from the Foreign and Commonwealth Office, the Department of Health, the Home Office and the Nigerian Government), and a West African Offenders Practice Issues Group. The latter provides a forum for UK professionals, voluntary sector representatives, and the Nigerian High commission to appraise policy and practice issues that affect Nigerian nationals in particular, and foreign offenders in general.

Establishing a framework for dialogue

The Criminal Justice Act 1991, the Children Act 1989, the UN Convention of the Rights of The Child and the White Paper 'Custody Care and Justice' provided building blocks for recognising the legal, social and welfare requirements of foreign nationals in British prisons. Furthermore, when taken as a whole, the policy frameworks that underpin these instruments confronted legal and penal philosophies that have hitherto prevented consideration being given to the children of foreign nationals. Granting recognition to the rights of children whose parents are imprisoned forcefully challenges the very notions of 'innocence', 'justice' and 'guilt' upon which both legal and penal policy has traditionally been constructed.

Against the background of this policy framework and in light of Penny Green's observation that over 73 per cent of Nigerian women in prison have children (and 23 per cent of whom have 5 or more children), the challenge for the British and the Nigerian Governments is to determine how justice is served by separating Nigerian nationals from their children, and whether imprisoning hundreds of Nigerian nationals in the UK serves any meaningful purpose.

Notes

1. Penny Green, *Drug Couriers*, Howard League for Penal Reform, July 1991.
2. New figures released by the Nigerian Population Commission in March 1992 put the population figure at 88.5 million, which is 35 million less than the estimates of the United Nations and the World Bank.

3
Drug Couriers: Discourses, Perceptions and Policies

Rosa del Olmo

Introduction

More than sixty years ago, US sociologists W. I. Thomas and F. Swaine Thomas demonstrated that when situations are defined as real, they are real in their consequences, even if the definition is absurd.[1] Recalling this proposition, the Spanish sociologist Emilio Lamo de Espinosa, when referring to the field of drugs, wrote: 'The way in which drugs are defined and perceived has fundamental consequences, because the important thing is not what is happening, but rather what is thought to be happening.'[2] The Dutch social psychologist Peter Cohen stated elsewhere: 'I could not help but seeing much of what happened around me in the drug arena as social constructions, realities created by a myriad of relationships between persons who use concepts to understand a reality that would adapt them for their survival within these relationships'.[3]

Other authors have indicated the importance of studying the construction of the various discourses that attempt to explain specific social problems, and their possible repercussions on the resolution or exacerbation of those problems. Along this line of thought, I consider that any attempt to approach the field of drugs must take into account the importance of language and specifically the words which are used in discourse construction. Discourse is an essential element in building perception and in the construction of any social reality which eventually serves to legitimize State policy.

In this sense, discourses are never neutral, but part of the reality conditioning them. At the same time, reality reinforces the context of discourses. The selection of one type of linguistic sign reflects the ways of perceiving and interpreting the world of whoever uses the language.[4] As a result, language has its effects on conforming subjectivity and constructing reality.

Moreover, regarding drugs there is a need to examine the *symbolic* role played by those who make the rules – that is, lawyers and medical doctors – those Howard Becker called 'moral entrepreneurs'[5] – in their capacity to organize the observers' perceptions, attitudes and feelings by means of 'crusades' against what they perceive as evil.[6] But it is also important to take into account the *legitimizing* role played by those who apply the rules – that is, the different security forces charged with implementing policies, who may be called 'repression entrepreneurs'. Last but not least, there is a need to examine the *amplifying* role of 'media entrepreneurs', in their capacity to reinforce a discourse by spreading its contents through various means.

There is a symbiosis between the symbolic aspects of moral entrepreneurs – to end vice and sin – and the instrumental interests of repression entrepreneurs – to amplify their realm of competence.[7] At the same time, moral entrepreneurs become mediators between public feelings and law creation, while repression entrepreneurs mediate between law and concrete social situations, where law must be implemented.[8]

On the other hand, many contradictions and mistakes within the drug debate are related to semantic problems and specifically to the varied perceptions of scientific and international institutions.[9] However, its analysis is very complex due to the connection between scientific discourses, power relations and the exercise of social control.[10]

In other words, discourse production is oriented by social structure, embodying the central issues of power and control. Therefore, examining why and how we define and discuss a social problem is essentially a matter of power relationships.

In this respect, the final consolidation of the official/scientific drug discourse is a result of specific strategies, where international conferences play a key role in projecting for example, the anti-drugs movement.[11] In the present century, the US Government has been its promoter, through different discourses built to justify, in the international arena, the need to implement determinate policies. These policies have not been uniform but have changed as the perception of the drug problem has varied.

For example in the sixties, with the spread in the use of a variety of drugs, especially marijuana and hallucinogens among American middle class youth, the problem was perceived by US authorities as a social threat – that is, as 'a struggle between good and evil'. Those responsible for inciting consumption came from the ghettos and were labelled 'criminal', whilst the consumer came from different social circumstances and was labelled 'sick'. Meanwhile, the medical discourse created the *dependency stereotype* in relation to consumption and the juridical discourse the *criminal stereotype*. A double discourse emerged in the 1960s, which may be called the *medical-juridical discourse*. Being a hybrid of the two prevailing paradigms, this dual discourse established an ideology of differentiation, so necessary to distinguish between consumer and dealer, the sick and the criminal.[12]

But at the same time, in terms of 'national security', the geopolitical discourse's main concern was 'the internal enemy'. Policies were directed toward strengthening the Mental Health Industry, with different types of treatment experimentation, and toward developing operations for the control of US borders, such as the famous *Operation Intercept*, designed to stop the flow of drugs from Mexico.

Drugs in the 1980s

In the eighties, a radical change may be observed in the discourse, the perceptions and the policies implemented to deal with the drug phenomenon.

As the United States entered the 1980s, statistics revealed the largest number of drug consumers in the country's history, particularly of cocaine and marijuana. Thus, the 1984 National Strategy for Prevention of Drug Abuse and Drug Trafficking stated the following:

More than 20 million Americans use marijuana at least once a month. One out of 18 high school seniors use marijuana daily. Over four million people, half of whom are between the ages of 18 and 25, are current users of cocaine. Approximately one-half million Americans are heroin addicts. Countless others are affected by the significant abuse problems which involve medical drugs manufactured in illicit laboratories or diverted from legal pharmaceutical sources. Alcohol is a major problem as well; there are an estimated 10 million adult problem drinkers and an additional three million between the ages of 14 and 17.[13]

At the same time, that document pointed out, for the first time, that cocaine was 'as destructive to health as heroin'.[14]

By March 1981, President Reagan had already declared his concern with the drug problem: 'The improper use of drugs is one of our greatest problems. If we don't act, we run the risk of losing a large part of a whole generation', were his words. In February 1982, Reagan launched his 'War on Drugs' as an 'urgent matter of national security'.

Several factors contributed to this decision: the developmental capacity of the enterprise producing psychoactive substances considered illegal, their consolidation in transnational industries, their ability to involve several nation-states, but with capitals beyond any nation's control or interference, etc. Nevertheless, the central concern became *drugs originating from abroad* – and especially the *economic and political aspects* of the cocaine traffic.

The Reagan Administration's main priorities

1. Economics
The new emphasis given to drugs may be related to a series of events. For example, in terms of economics, it is significant that by 1980, the DEA had detected an important flight of capital to bank accounts outside the US, in amounts greater than $2 billion, deriving from cocaine and marijuana sales. Thirty one of the 250 banks in Miami facilitated this capital flight, with five of them belonging to 'narcotraffickers', who sent their money to Switzerland, Panama, the Bahamas, and other locations to be 'laundered' and reintroduced into the United States, through legitimate investments.[15]

34

Thus, it is logical that at the beginning of the 1980s, it was publicly announced that the DEA was changing its tactics 'increasingly concentrating on the *money* and the so-called *narcodollars*. By 1982, DEA's priorities were investigation and eradication of cocaine'.[16]

The new emphasis on the economic aspects of drugs – cocaine above all – was so apparent that even experts, previously involved in spreading the medical discourse gave credence to this new focus. For example, the well-known psychiatrist, Sidney Cohen, wrote:

> The public health aspects of cocaine are no longer considered grave, even though morbidity and mortality from cocaine are on the rise. It is the disorganizing aspects of billions of *cocadollars* in the producing and consuming nations that produces a level of corruption, violence, and demoralization that harms us all.[17]

Similarly, researchers from the National Institute for Drug Abuse – an organization notorious for spreading the medical discourse – also referred to these aspects in detail. According to Richard R. Clayton:

> There are two economic and political themes that must be taken into consideration. First, the macroeconomic estimates of the cocaine industry are calculated to be between $50 and $70 billion a year. *The amount of money that is moved* has to have a significant impact on the economic structure of our society. Second, there is the cost to US society from improper drug use in *terms of dollars* for treatment, hospitalization, and loss of productivity and profits due to illness, disability, death, crime, and other consequences of cocaine consumption ... *From a cold, rational, economic perspective*, loss of productivity and overall loss to society due to the premature death of a street heroin addict can be very low. This is even more true if the addict has been chronically unemployed, in and out of treatment and jail, frequently involved in criminality to support his/her habit. *On the other hand, think about the premature death from a cocaine overdose of a stockbroker, a public relations executive, or a lawyer from a large firm.* In this case, from the same perspective, *the loss to society is considerable.*[18]

This obvious economic concern sharpened during the Reagan Administration, and is reflected in a 1983 report of its Joint Committee on Economics, which pointed out that the underground economy in the US concealed $222 billion from the International Revenue Service, that is, 7.5 percent of the gross national product. Drugs alone were estimated to be a business of over $100 billion within the US, equivalent to 10 percent of the country's industrial production.

Among the first measures taken to counteract the underground economy were interagency investigations such as the successful *Operation Greenback*, mounted by the Treasury and Justice Departments in 1981. Its objective was to uncover irregular manipulations of the banks and intermediary financiers. At the same time, the Centre for Financial Law Enforcement was created, which channelled the information collected by the operatives.

However, the solution to the underground economy was not simple, due to the domestic problems in the country including inflation, the falling dollar and unemployment. It appeared to be necessary, above all, to control the underground economy outside US borders. One of the first measures taken in this respect was an amendment to the Posse Comitatus Act allowing the military to engage in civilian law enforcement. Executive Order No. 12333 authorized the US intelligence service to gather information on drug traffic abroad.

Drugs produced abroad should neither enter the US nor leave the producing country, according to the new protectionist economic policy of the Reagan Administration. Cocaine had become the most expensive and in terms of volume, the most significant of the imported drugs and as such demanded a new enforcement infrastructure.

In January 1982, the Cabinet Council on Legal Policy was set up to coordinate all efforts and was placed in the hands of George Bush. Further, the South Florida Task Force was set up as an initiative against criminal problems in Florida, including drug smuggling and illegal financial activities. In March 1983, President Reagan created the National Narcotics Border Interdiction System (NNBIS), overseen by George Bush, to coordinate interdiction efforts on US borders. The control programme for the Caribbean region was implemented, with collaboration of the DEA, US

Customs, the Coast Guard, and technical support from the Armed Forces.

In 1983, Congress also passed the Comprehensive Crime Control Act, which contained new measures to combat drug trafficking and organized crime, and the Gilman-Hawkins Amendment, which suspended economic aid to countries that did not cooperate with the US anti-drug programme. International cooperation with US control programmes increased in line with one of the basic goals of the new strategy: to internationalize drug control. In this regard, a series of operations was carried out including: *Operation Sword Fish* in south Florida; *Operation Trap* in the Caribbean in 1982; and in 1983, *Operation Godfather* against cocaine in Colombia, Mexico and other countries and *Operation Hat Trick* in the Caribbean.

During this decade, central policy emphasis turned to law enforcement. In 1973, the DEA had 1,423 agents and a budget of $74.9 million. By 1985, it had 2,429 agents and a budget of $359.5 million. In general, the federal government spent £708 million on law enforcement in 1981, and $1.2 billion in 1985. In contrast, the Department of Education's programme budget decreased from $404 million in 1981 to $253 million in 1985.

At the same time, Reagan assigned the Armed Forces and policy services greater participation in national defence against drug traffic. Under his administration the military's anti-drug budget grew from less than $5 million in 1982 to over $200 million in 1988 (WOLA, 1991: 18). The President perceived the international drug trade as a problem of *national security*, and formally declared it so when signing National Security Decision Directive #221 in April 1986.

2. Politics

Since the early 1980s blame for the drug problem was placed on supply – that is on traffic, which explains that the discourse became directed towards the *external enemy*, as the only guilty party.

In order to legitimize the new policies and to strengthen the image of an *external enemy*, the word 'drugs' was phased out and replaced by the term 'narcotics', used earlier when drugs were associated with opiates. Only now it was adapted to cocaine, despite the fact that this drug is technically a stimulant and not à narcotic. Beginning in the 1980s, the 'media entrepreneurs' broadcast this terminology on a hemispheric level, propagating the term *narcotraffic*, through a clever continental campaign of massive diffusion, which soon became synonymous with all stages of the cocaine trade, before the drug's arrival in the US.

This new discourse, with its geopolitical content, no longer established a distinction between the sick-consumer and criminal-trafficker, rather the juxtaposition was between *victim* and *victimizer countries*. The US was thus presented as the victim country *par excellence*, the main target of *narcotraffickers'*. And 'narcotics' were referred to in terms of a 'plague' invading the country. Subsequently, when the problem of consumption was internationalized in the discourse, it was extended to other countries which also became victims.

But for Reagan a priority – as important or more than drugs – was to launch the counterinsurgency war in Latin America to prevent any attempt to follow the Cuban model and, after 1980, Nicaragua's Sandinista movement. By labelling drugs a *national security* problem, it was possible to connect both priorities: counterinsurgency and drugs. A new discourse appeared – more complex, but more consistent with the current objectives. It was the *transnational political juridical discourse* (which may also be called *geopolitical discourse*) according with the advent of the geopolitical control model and the incorporation of National Security Doctrine's postulates into the drug theme.

However, the use of the term *narcotraffic*, to refer to the 'enemy' outside the United States, was not easily accepted by all governments until the term *narcoguerrilla*, and later *narcoterrorism*, emerged to deal with the political aspects of the problem. The *Latin American political-criminal stereotype* was then accepted as 'a reality'.

Cuba and Nicaragua were presented as victimizing countries, accused of being accomplices in drug trafficking and the promotion of *narcotraffic* in Latin American countries, through support of the *narcoguerrilla*. In South America, the victimizing discourse was directed particularly against the Colombian M-19 and FARC movements, and later against the Peruvian Shining Path movement. The *Latin American political-criminal stereotype* ceased to be the exclusive domain of US domestic rhetoric and acquired a hemispheric character.

First, reference was made to the Cuban Connection, with concrete accusations made by the State Department against Cuban government functionaries living in Colombia connecting the transport of weapons to the M-19 with marijuana traffic to the US aided by the Cuban government.

The news media unleashed a continental campaign against Cuba, which sharpened in 1984 and 1985, when Nicaragua was included to link the governments of both countries to major Colombian drug traffickers. Later attempts were made to tie guerrilla groups operating in various countries to the drug trade. This perception contributed to the legitimation of US government aid to the counter-revolutionary Nicaraguan *contras*.

The geopolitical discourse was then broadened to include regional governments as possible *victimizers*. In 1986, when a campaign against Mexico was unleashed and later extended to Panama, the US government affirmed in the news that 'the US must avoid collaboration with government functionaries in countries such as Panama, which have proven ties with *narcotraffic*' – a clear example of media discourse's function, given the wide public acceptance of General Noriega's later capture.

A further connection between counterinsurgency and drugs was possible after 1986, with the Pentagon's development of Low-intensity Conflict Doctrine, where drugs were considered as one of its main missions. In this respect, *Operation Blast Furnace*, launched in Bolivia in July 1986, was the first US military operation in support of counter-narcotics activities in the Andes, followed in 1987 by *Operation Snowcap*, where paramilitary tactics were used for the first time.

Despite resistance from important members of the Defence Department to military participation in the 'War on Drugs', a series of events conducted by the Pentagon created the conditions for later acceptance of military participation in 'anti-drug missions'.[19]

Parallel to the events characterizing the 1980s in the US, the same discourse proliferated at the official level in Latin America and a series of measures, prioritizing the drug problem, were adopted there. The discourse sought to blur differences between consuming and producing nations in order to highlight that 'the drug vice is a plague that reaches everywhere' and in that way involve Latin American governments in President Reagan's 'War on Drugs'. International conferences played a key role here and, particularly, the new perception that the drug problem was a 'shared responsibility' of all the countries and 'a threat to democracy'. In this respect, it is important to remember two initiatives of the Organisation of American states: the Specialized International Conference against Drug Trafficking, held in Rio de Janeiro, Brazil, 22–24 April 1985 (where the only drug discussed was cocaine) and Guatemala's 'Alliance of the Americas against Narcotraffic' organised in November 1986.

Thus, after 1986, the new perception was well entrenched, but it is also necessary to recall here the approval in October of the Anti-Drug Abuse Act (PL 99–570) – and later on the Anti-Drug Abuse Act (PL 100–690) of 1988 – where the process, commonly referred to as *certification* came into effect.[20] The importance of involving other countries in Reagan's 'War on Drugs' was crucial, if we recall that certification establishes a direct relationship between American assistance to major illicit drug producing and transit countries and their positive performance on drug control:

> . . . If the President fails to certify a country, or if the Congress disapproves a certification, the United States must withhold most economic and military assistance, along with support for World Bank and other loans.[21]

Military escalation under Bush

When George Bush became President of the United States in 1989, drugs were perceived as the country's foremost problem. An intense level of alarm over cocaine-related problems, promoted by 'media entrepreneurs' at the time, was pervasive in US society. In August, a poll in New York favoured the use of troops abroad in the fight against drugs. Thus, the National Drug Control Strategy, presented by President Bush on 5 September 1989, proposed a significant escalation of the war.

Upon taking office, President Bush began to lay the legal groundwork for increased military action abroad in the drugs war. So in August, he signed National Security Directive #18, authorizing armed forces personnel to go beyond 'security areas' in narcotic-related programs abroad, essentially permitting troops to enter areas of potential conflict with guerrillas or traffickers. In September, the new National Defence Authorization Act gave the Department of Defence the responsibility to act as the chief federal agency for the detection and monitoring of aerial and maritime transit of illegal drugs into the US. In October, General Colin Powell took command as head of the Joint Chiefs of Staff and fully supported a greater engagement of the armed forces in countering drug trafficking. Also, General Maxwell Thurman became head of SouthCom in Panama, becoming the military's renowed 'drug warrior'. In November, the US Department of Justice Office of Legal Counsel issued a legal opinion that US military personnel could arrest foreign citizens in other countries.[22]

Thus, Bush's 'war on drugs' sharply escalated the reliance on US and foreign armed forces to fight that war, and *Operation Just Cause*, launched in Panama against General Noriega, in December 1989, was the first evidence. As a result, Bush's anti-narcotics programme was the most expensive in US history. Spending on all federal anti-drug programmes increased from $6.4 billion in 1988 to over $11 billion in 1992.[23]

The Washington Office on Latin America explains this turn to the military in the following terms:

As domestic pressure for action against drug abuse rose throughout the 1980s, Congress and the administration expressed frustration at the failure of federal anti-narcotic measures. Members of Congress from both parties called for the increased use of the military. And within 'source countries', US officials encountered a host of obstacles, including fears that paramilitary police efforts were inadequate in the face of well-armed cartels, especially in situations where civil conflicts complicated the scenario.[24]

Therefore, the Strategy's international measures differ greatly from previous strategies. As Raphael F.Perl, member of the US Congress Research Service, pointed out: 'A shift in emphasis may be observed from a focus on disrupting the coca farmers and producers to a focus on disrupting the activities of the traffickers, if possible at their major points of vulnerability'.[25] The same author summarizes the new policy in the following terms:

1. There is for the first time, support for limited economic assistance to the main cocaine-producing countries:

2. Greater emphasis on disrupting and dismantling trafficking operations (destroying laboratories, seizing chemical precursors, confiscating property) and less on destruction of farming activities (crop eradication);

3. It encourages greater levels of participation by Andean armed forces in anti-drug operations;

4. Provides for an increase in support by US armed forces to repressive agencies in countries throughout the continent; and

5. Improves intelligence operations.[26]

The Strategy called for a Presidential Summit among coca-producing countries in order to reach an agreement between the US and the Andean region on US goals and strategies in the region.[27] This objective was accomplished on 15 February, 1990, with the signing of the *Cartagena Declaration* by the Presidents of Bolivia, Colombia, Peru and the United States, which laid the foundation for consolidating the *Andean Initiative*, designed to emphasize military, economic and law-enforcement aid to Bolivia, Colombia and Peru at a cost of $2.2 billion over five years.

Nevertheless, the consolidation of the *Andean Initiative* was not easy. National definitions and perceptions, as to the nature of the drug problem, and the policies to be implemented varied. The US government viewed it in terms of law-enforcement requiring military intervention, while Andean governments viewed drug production and control as an economic and social issue requiring trade benefits. However, US policies were imposed. The escalation of the war to cover the whole continent and the Panama-based US Southern Command 1990's declaration regarding drugs as its 'number one priority', were followed by the Pentagon's installation of a sophisticated regional intelligence network, which draws on satellites, air reconnaissance flights and radar based in 18 countries.[28]

Drugs in the 1990s

By the nineties, key changes may be observed in drugs discourse, perception and politics. Beyond the growing complexity of the phenomenon, those changes may be related to the end of the Cold War and the development of the so-called 'post-cold war era'. The New World Order and recent global changes converts the US drug problem into part of a collective challenge that confronts the world due to 'the multinational nature of the threat',[29] a position already expressed in the 1991 US National Drug Control Strategy when referring to the international drug trade as 'a threat to our national security and the security and stability of other nations'.[30] Along the same lines, the General Assembly of the United Nations proclaimed the period from 1991 to 2000 the United Nations Decade against Drug Abuse to promote the implementation of it *Global Programme of Action*, adopted on 23 February 1990.

Drug trafficking is no longer considered only as a 'criminal activity', but rather as a 'commodity trade conducted by transnational consortiums', which are able to operate successfully only by interacting with and blending into already established legitimate markets. Moreover, the drug business is compared to a modern multinational corporation with the necessary ingredients to conduct a successful international enterprise, such as global reach and a creative, flexible organizational culture.[31] There is the perception that, in the long run, the only truly effective way to suppress the drug trade and its traffickers is by reducing global demand. Thus, the current model for supply reduction must give way to a greater emphasis on demand control. This view was exemplified by President Bush who, when speaking at the Opening Plenary Session of the San Antonio Drug Summit, 22 February, 1992, said that 'drugs are an international plague caused by both consumer and supplier'.

As the main concern of the nineties is with the global economy, the new official discourse can be identified as a *transnational economic discourse*, complemented by a geopolitical discourse in terms of a *global enemy*. Meanwhile, a scientific discourse emerges in terms of 'world health', where prevention, education and treatment become priorities.

In close connection with these discourses, we find the perception of an increase in consumption of all type of drugs by younger people. At the same time, the drug user is no longer a 'victim'. The 1992 US National Drug Control Strategy clearly stated that 'the drug problem reflects bad decisions by individuals with free wills'.[32]

In geopolitical terms, the perception of the *global enemy* widens to include Colombian 'cartels' – especially Cali's, international organized crime, the Russian 'mafia' and various terrorist groups. The main concern is with their capacity to set up sophisticated financial networks that move the money into and through the legal financial system to conceal its origins, as a result of the revolution under way in the global financial and banking markets.[33] At the same time, present policy views cocaine as the most threatening of the various illegal drugs, despite the fact that in the official discourse all drugs, including tobacco and alcohol, are mentioned.

In this respect, the 1992 US National Drug Control Strategy gives primary emphasis to the disruption of the drug organizations at their home country base of operations, through 'the destruction of the trafficking infrastructure, the investigation, prosecution, punishment, and, where appropriate, extradition of drug traffickers and money launderers; the seizure of drugs and assets; and the destruction of processing and shipping facilities'.[34] In the same terms, the United Nations Convention Against Illicit Traffic in Narcotic Drugs and Psychotropic Substances, adopted in Vienna on 19 December, 1988, gives priority to confiscation and extradition.

In other words, the fear that drug organizations might control the banking system and launder vast sums of money through it has become the nineties' main policy concern. This creates a new *financial stereotype*.

The growing importance of the transnational economy in the official drugs' discourse may be supported by the persistence of global multilateral initiatives to reach international cooperation against money laundering. A series of Government agreements have been signed, and growing importance is given to this topic in most international conferences' agendas. Specialized bodies have emerged such as the Financial Action Task Force (first convened by the seven major industrial nations in 1989) which, in 1991, set up a five-year programme to achieve a broad-based international

44

agreement on cooperative action against money laundering; and the Experts Group created by the Organisation of American States to draft a model anti-money laundering statute, already adopted by its General Assembly in 1992.

Despite the fact that President Clinton's National Drug Control Strategy attempted to give priority to domestic problems, increasing prevention and treatment facilities, while changing 'the way international programmes are considered',[35] all the evidence seems to indicate that current discourses, perceptions and policies are directed towards a global drug control strategy which minimizes national differences.

It is too soon to determine the outcome of this new approach, but it raises one central question: if drug control and specifically justice becomes global and extra-territorial, what will become of national justice systems and army and police forces? And perhaps more important, who will lead this new development and under which discourse and whose perception?

Notes

1. Thomas, W. I. and D. S., *The Child in America: Behaviour Problems and Programmes*, A. A. Knopf, New York, 1928.
2. Lamo de Espinosa E., *Delitos sin victima. Orden Social y ambivalencia moral*, Alianza Editorial, Madrid, 1989.
3. Cohen, P., *Drugs as a Social Construct*, Universiteit van Amsterdam, Amsterdam, 1990.
4. Bolivar, A., *El encuentro de dos mundos a traves del discurso*, UCV, Caracas, 1992.
5. Becker, H., *Outsiders: Studies in the Sociology of Deviance*, The Free Press, New York, 1963, p. 147.
6. Cloyd, J. W., *Drogas y Control de Informacion*, Ediciones Tres Tiempos, Buenos Aires, 1982, p. 70.
7. Lamo de Espinosa, op. cit., p. 33.
8. Cloyd, op. cit., p. 132.
9. Arnao, G., *Proibito Capire: Proibionismo e Politiche di Controllo Sociale*, Edizioni Gruppo Abele, Torino 1990, pp. 21–22
10. Morrisey, E. R., 'Power and Control through discourse. The case of drinking and drinking problems among women', *Contemporary Crises*, Volume 10, No. 2, p. 157.
11. Cloyd, op. cit., p. 76.
12. del Olmo, R., 'The Hidden Face of Drugs', *Social Justice*, Vol. 18, No. 4, p. 18.
13. The White House, *National Strategy for the Prevention of Drug Abuse and Drug Trafficking*, US Government Printing Office, Washington DC 1984, p. 6.
14. Ibid., p. 6.

15. Conde, P., 'El Triangulo de las Bermudas de la Cocaina', *Interview*, No. 10 474, June 1985, p. 30.
16. Beck, M. and Shannon, E., 'A New Attack on Drugs', *Newsweek*, 20 July 1981, p. 30 (emphasis added).
17. Cohen, S., *Cocaine: the Bottom Line*, The American Council for Drug Education, Washington DC 1985, p. 8.
18. Clayton, R. R., 'Cocaine Use in the US: In a Blizzard or Just Being Snowed', *Cocaine Use in America: Epidemiologic and Clinical Perspectives*, NIDA Research Monograph Series 61, Washington DC 1985, pp. 14–15.
19. For example, the Conference on 'Low Intensity War' held at the Pentagon on January 14–15, 1986; the creation of the Army-Airforce Centre for Low Intensity Conflict, the principal think-tank on low intensity conflict within the Armed Forces, at Langley, Virginia; and the publication in August 1991 of the Final Report of the Low Intensity Conflict Joint Project, which specifies concepts, strategy and application of the Low Intensity Conflict War doctrine in the Third World. Note also the further militarisation of drug control through the establishment of the Florida-based Board for Low Intensity Conflict at the National Security Council in 1987.
    See Washington Office on Latin America (WOLA), *Clear and Present Dangers: The US Military and the War on Drugs in the Andes*, Washington DC, October 1991, pp. 35 and 138.
20. Perl, R. F., 'The US Congress International Drug Policy and the Anti-Drug Abuse Act of 1988', *Journal of Interamerican Studies and World Affairs*, Vol. 30, No. 2–3, Summer 1988.
21. The White House, *National Drug Control Strategy*, US Government Printing Office, Washington DC, 1989, pp. 68–69.
22. WOLA, op. cit., p. 19.
23. ibid., pp. 6–7.
24. ibid., p. 7.
25. Perl, op. cit., p. 134.
26. ibid., p. 24.
27. The White House, 1989, op. cit., p. 63.
28. WOLA, op. cit., p. 1.
29. Centre for Strategic and International Studies, *The Transnational Drug Challenge and the New World Order*, Washington DC, part ix.
30. The White House, 1991, op. cit., p. 77.
31. Centre for Strategic Studies, op. cit., p. 9.
32. The White House, 1992, op. cit., p. 2.
33. Centre for Strategic Studies, op. cit., pp. 11–12.
34. The White House 1992, op. cit., p. 80.
35. The White House, *National Drug Control Strategy: Recovering our communities from drugs and violence*, US Government Printing Office, Washington DC, 1994, part iv.

4
Prisoners of War:
Women drug couriers in the United States

Tracy Huling[1]

Introduction

Drug couriers are a key target of drug enforcement efforts and subject to harsh sentencing policies across the globe, yet only limited information on them is available.

A review of the small but emerging body of international literature on drug couriers suggests that women drug couriers should be of special concern to the criminal justice community internationally.[2] Specific information on women arrested and imprisoned for international drug importation/exportation is sparse, but what is available suggests that women's participation in transporting narcotics across national borders increased dramatically to become significant during the past decade.

Latin American criminologist Rosa del Olmo cites the National Police of Colombia's 1984 annual report's finding of an overall increase in female participation in cocaine trafficking, from 184 women in 1983 to 802 in 1984, especially as *mules*, or drug couriers. She states that 'an examination of the remainder of the continent's geography yields similar figures'.[3]

A survey of foreign nationals imprisoned in Great Britain between June and November 1988 for illegal drug importation found that 35 percent were women. When broken out by type of drug imported, the proportion of women was even higher for cocaine (50 percent) and cannabis (48 percent).[4]

In her groundbreaking study on drug couriers imprisoned in Britain, Penny Green found a large increase in the number of women found guilty of drug importation/exportation offences between 1986 and 1987, as well as a slight decrease in the number of men found guilty during the same period. She found slight increases for both men and women between 1988 and 1989.[5]

Of a subsequent sample of 149 drug importation cases awaiting disposition in Britain between 1 September 1991 and 30 April 1992, 33.6 percent were identified as female.[6]

It should therefore come as no surprise that female drug couriers constitute a significant portion of the population in female prisons in the countries for which data is available. Van Putten reports that 30 percent of the inmates at the Amsterdam Penitentiary for Women are couriers.[7] Penny Green found that approximately 20 percent of the female prison population in Britain between 1986 and 1989 were drug couriers, while male couriers accounted for only 4 percent of the population in men's prisons during the same period.[8]

According to Rosa del Olmo, a high percentage of the women in prison in Latin America in July 1987 were detained or sentenced under drug trafficking laws: 62 percent in Cuenca, Ecuador; 40 percent in Guayaquil, Ecuador; 28 percent in Rio de Janeiro, Brazil; 51 percent in Caracas, Venezuela; and 43 percent in Los Teques, Venezuela.[9]

The lack of repatriation treaties between most drug-demand countries and drug-supply countries means that couriers who are foreign nationals end up serving lengthy prison sentences in the country of arrest. Thousands of miles away from family and friends, ignorant of the laws and criminal justice systems in the countries where they are prosecuted and incarcerated, and often unable to speak the language in their new 'home', many foreign couriers face a host of unique problems.

In a review of federally sentenced women in Canada, Margaret Shaw discusses the circumstances of women couriers:

The situation of women convicted for trafficking receives little attention ... partly because those who are non-Canadians have little support from or contact with the community. A number of them have difficulties with language, and [tenuous] contact with their families. .... They receive much longer and 'deterrent' sentences than almost all other offenders. . . . In almost all cases they acted as couriers, while the organisers for whom such sentences are primarily intended were not located. [T]hey had hoped to find a way out of their financial difficulties. Whether or not they were aware of what they were doing, such women find themselves with sentences of up to 12 years for agreeing to carry packages through Customs. They have usually never been in contact with the law before.[10]

National sentencing policies that tie sanctions to drug amounts and limit judicial consideration of mitigating factors also disparately affected women, who tend to play marginal roles in drug trafficking, have little if any prior criminal history, and often are the sole caretakers of young children.

The separation of women from their children as a result of the lengthy incarceration of drug couriers is, according to most published information, nothing less than devastating for mothers and children. In Britain, Tarzi and Hedge's analysis of the differences in marital status between male and female couriers with dependent children strongly suggests that the impact of incarceration on families is more profound when the incarcerated family member is a woman. Of the foreign national couriers sentenced to imprisonment at London's Isleworth Crown Court between June and November 1988, 75 percent of the women were single, divorced, or widowed, with an average of three dependents each. In comparison, only 32 percent of the men were single, widowed, or divorced, and they served as a single parent to, on average, 0.48 dependents each.

Documenting the experience in the United States

At the request of a chaplain at the women's jail on Riker's Island, New York in 1991, I began documenting the stories of women arrested at New York City's John F. Kennedy Airport for smuggling drugs into the United States. Many of the women claimed they were innocent, that they had been tricked into acting as drug mules by people who planted drugs in their belongings or they had been coerced by threats of violence and death, either to themselves or loved ones. Those who said they were indeed guilty presented evidence of hard times – a small business in danger of folding; a husband who left with the money and without the children – or of 'duties' as the sister, daughter, or wife of a drug dealer.

The women I spoke with were of all colours, nationalities, and ages, but there were some things they had in common. All lacked any history of involvement with the criminal justice system and all were terrified of the realities of life on Riker's Island. There were no 'career criminals' looking forward to 'three hots and a cot'. Most were despondent and frightened for children left behind, sometimes thousands of miles and an ocean or two away. All had been charged with possession of four ounces or more of a narcotic drug, an A-I felony in New York that carries a mandatory minimum prison sentence of fifteen years to life, the same penalty faced by murderers, arsonists, and kidnappers.

The first group of women interviewed were part of a large influx of drug mules (most female) turned over by federal authorities to New York State for prosecution. Until 1990, most airport cases involving heroin and cocaine were prosecuted under federal law. As the federal courts and prisons became jammed with such cases and the federal judiciary rebelled, more and more cases were dumped on the states.

In 1990 the US Attorney for the Eastern District, who has jurisdiction over JFK Airport, raised the threshold quantity of drugs for federal prosecution for heroin from 250 grams to 750 grams and for cocaine, from 1 kilo to 3 kilos. Such policy changes are made at the discretion of the individual federal prosecutor and may vary from district to district and from day to day.

The impact of such a policy change can mean, as it did for New York, the sudden appearance of hundreds of new drug cases that must be processed at the local level. Although this also results in a shift of costs from the federal government to states and localities, the political advantages to local prosecutors can be significant when such cases show up on computers and in election literature as serious felony convictions. Ironically, for the accused whose cases are no longer considered serious enough for federal jurisdiction, the switch to state prosecution can trigger harsher penalties than the ones they would have faced under federal law.

Some of the women's stories

- **Marie**, a 40–year-old black woman, carried with her on a plane from Haiti a small wooden statue filled with cocaine. She said she did it at the behest of a village police chief who told her he would blow up her mother's house with a grenade should she leave the country without the statue.

- **Delia**, a divorced mother of four with a seventh-grade education, travelled outside Greensboro, North Carolina, for the first time in her life to meet her future husband in Nigeria, the brother of a businessman she knew. The businessman, who paid for her plane ticket, had invited Delia to meet his brother, a doctor in Nigeria who was looking for an American wife. Delia's fiancé sent her home from Nigeria with a gift: a quilted suede coat, the lining of which she was told upon her arrest contained fifteen ounces of heroin.

- Twenty-five-year-old **Verna**, college educated and a management trainee at a bank in New York City, fell in love with a man who took her to meet his family in Jamaica. Packing for the return trip, Verna's boyfriend presented her with a longline brassière padded with drugs to wear back on the plane. When she tried to refuse, her boyfriend threatened her with a gun.

- **Blanca** was a mother of two and wife of a Colombian bartender who left her pregnant and ill with a gallbladder problem. Denied welfare benefits because she had a house, she tried factory piecework to make ends meet, but she soon fell behind in the mortgage payments. Approached by someone from her neighbourhood who knew of her problems, she agreed to carry a package of cocaine back from Colombia in exchange for $3,000.

- **Sonia**, a legal immigrant living in Miami with her husband and children, visited a brother in Haiti who had been stabbed. When she was told during her visit that her family in Haiti would be killed if she did not transport drugs back to the United States with her, she complied, she said, because 'Haiti is a very violent country'. Facing the prospect of being separated from her children for a minimum of fifteen to twenty-five years if she went to trial and lost, Sonia explored a plea bargain but was told that the alternative to going to trial was deportation to Haiti after a shortened prison sentence. Whatever the outcome of her case, Sonia figured she would never see her children again, and she suffered a nervous breakdown. Imprisoned on remand for almost three years in New York, Sonia resided in a secure psychiatric facility on heavy medication after she could no longer be maintained at Riker's. She had no history of mental illness prior to her arrest.

- **Robin** was found guilty at a jury trial of bringing two pounds of cocaine into the United States from Aruba, where she was vacationing with her boyfriend. A battered woman who mounted an affirmative defence of duress and provided eyewitness testimony, police reports, medical photographs, and copies of previous orders of protection, Robin said she carried the drugs because her boyfriend of twelve years threatened her with physical violence and abandonment in Aruba with no money or return airline ticket.

Breaking the silence

My first interviews with women drug mules followed almost a year of failed attempts by Sister Marion Defeis, the Catholic chaplain at Riker's Island Women's Facility, to interest state and city officials, prosecutors, defence attorneys, and foreign consulates in the plight of these women. She got few responses. Those who did respond said that New York's 'Rockefeller' Drug Laws tied their hands.

Enacted in 1973, the Rockefeller Drug Laws contain some of the country's most severe penalties for drug sale and possession. Life imprisonment is mandatory for persons possessing as little as two ounces of a preparation or mixture containing a narcotic drug or selling as small a quantity as half an ounce. The penalties apply without regard to the circumstances of the offence, the offender's character or background, or whether the person is a first-time or repeat offender.

Sister Marion found that there was some sympathy for street

dealers who had to take the rap for major traffickers, and for people in poor economic circumstances who voluntarily smuggle drugs in exchange for paltry sums of money. No-one connected with law enforcement, however, would acknowledge the possibility that a person could be duped or coerced into carrying drugs across an international border.

Developing the research

In 1991, the Correctional Association of New York agreed to support my research on the circumstances of women arrested at JFK Airport and to oversee production of a thirty-minute documentary film examining their treatment by the criminal justice system. At the time, no academic research had been done on drug couriers in the United States and no information on this group of offenders had been published by government sources. To break through the wall of silence and apathy surrounding these women, both the criminal justice community and the public required accurate information on drug couriers.

For the Correctional Association study, published in 1992,[11] anecdotal information was collected through interviews with the accused women, prosecutors, defence attorneys, drug enforcement agents, and Customs officials. Statistics provided by the Queen's County district attorney's office were analysed for fifty-nine cases disposed of in Queen's County between January 1990 and December 1991 that involved women arrested at JFK Airport for drug smuggling. Also analysed were data supplied by the New York State Department of Criminal Justice Services on the dispositions of all A-I drug arrests in New York City between 1986 and 1990.

The major findings of the statistical analysis include:

- The overwhelming majority (96 percent) of women arrested at JFK Airport for drug smuggling, charged with A-I drug felonies, and sentenced to *life terms* in prison under New York's Rockefeller Drug Laws, had no prior criminal record.

- Very few of these women (5 percent) were convicted at trial. Most (95 percent) plea bargained to a reduced charge, the vast majority to A-II felonies, which carry a mandatory minimum of three years to life.

- A significant number of the fifty-nine women sampled spent many months in New York City jails as unconvicted defendants.[12]

- As a result of the 1990 decision by the US Attorney for the Eastern District to raise the threshold quantity of drugs for federal prosecution, there was a dramatic rise (192 percent) in the number of women arrested in Queen's County (the county with jurisdiction over JFK Airport arrests) on A-I drug felony charges between 1989 and 1990. This increase was far greater than that experienced by any other New York City borough,[13] and far greater than the increase for similarly situated men in Queen's County (48 percent).

- In terms of absolute numbers of women arrested and imprisoned for A-I drug felonies between 1986 and 1990, Queen's County outranked all other boroughs in New York City. A greater proportion of women arrested for A-I drug felonies were sent to prison in Queen's County than in any other borough.

- Application of the Rockefeller Drug Laws in Queen's County appears to have had a disproportionate impact on Hispanic women. The majority of women arrested in Queen's County for A-I felonies (whose cases were disposed of between 1986 and 1990) shared a similar background – that is, they held no prior criminal record and were disproportionately Hispanic, compared with white or black women. Nevertheless, they were sentenced to state prison as a consequence of these arrests. Of the white women charged, 50 percent were sentenced to prison; of the black women, 52 percent went to prison. The proportion of Hispanic women imprisoned was 83 percent.

The context of the research

Although the statistical findings of the research are evocative, their significance can only be realised fully when set in the context of the qualitative information collected through interviews.

All sectors of the criminal justice community recognised that the vast majority of women sent to New York State prisons as a result of A-I drug felony charges under New York's Rockefeller Drug Laws are neither career criminals nor drug 'queenpins'. Many members of this community, including police officers, judges, prosecutors, and defence attorneys, stated that despite this knowledge, they can apply neither the principles of justice nor the principles of rational sentencing to these women because of the Rockefeller Drug Laws' provisions.

Prosecutors said that because the charge is tied to the weight of the drug, they have no choice but to pursue A-I indictments for anyone found in possession of four ounces or more of an illegal drug. Once the A-I indictment is secured (and it almost always is), the lowest plea allowed under the current law is to an A-II felony. The only way around that is for a defendant to provide 'material assistance' leading to the arrest of a drug dealer, which can bring the sentence down to lifetime probation.

Most prosecutors and drug enforcement agents interviewed indicated that women can rarely offer material assistance of any value because they are involved so marginally, if at all, in the larger drug operation.[14]

Legal aid lawyers and court-appointed attorneys representing most of these women say they are extremely reluctant to risk a prison sentence of fifteen to twenty-five years to life for their clients by taking these cases to trial, particularly in the light of the acknowledged biases of juries in drug cases. According to some criminal defence attorneys, the complexity and expense of mounting a defence based on duress or the client's lack of knowledge works to discourage trials of individuals who claim they were duped or coerced.

Even if judges believe that the women were used by drug dealers, or coerced, or otherwise bear minimal culpability, they must sentence according to the mandatory dictates of the law. The number of 'illegal' sentences by judges seeking a way to avoid imposing irrational sanctions on some deserving defendants has increased substantially in recent years, but no judge I spoke with believed these individual acts of conscience could or should be viewed as effective reform.

From the perspective of the women interviewed who were charged and/or imprisoned under these laws, 'there is no justice in Athens'. They have been twice victimized, once by a drug dealer and again by the law.

Most of the women described situations where neither prosecutors nor defence attorneys investigated or even showed much interest in the circumstances under which they came to have drugs in their possession. Rather, they were told to 'cop a plea' because neither judge nor jury would believe their stories; where they were pressed into making decisions about pleading or going to trial without sufficient time to consider or consult with family members and lacking even a basic understanding of the law or of how the criminal justice system works.

Women told of being intimidated by impatient defenders, and they expressed confusion and despair about being advised to 'lie to the judge'. Many who claimed to have been duped or coerced into carrying drugs said they eventually pleaded guilty, because they were told that if they did not they would be sentenced to between 25 years and life, and their concern for children and families left behind drove them to take the offer of less time spent away from their loved ones.

The impact of the research

One of the outcomes of this research was the production of a video documentary, *Drug Mules* (1992), produced by the Correctional Association of New York, Inc. and Oz Films. It was first screened at Time Warner headquarters in Manhattan before an audience of one hundred representatives of local, state, and federal criminal justice agencies, journalists, and influential citizens. The screening had a significant impact. NBC broadcast a two-part news series on women drug couriers at Riker's, and feature stories and opinion columns ran in two major New York dailies. Prominent New Yorkers formed a committee to meet with the Queen's County district attorney, and the governor finally responded to a letter from Riker's Sister Marion written almost a year earlier.

The publicity generated several requests for additional screenings of the documentary, including one from Federal Judge Jack Weinstein, who in 1993 announced his refusal to continue to preside over drug cases at the federal level. Another came from the head of the Bronx County Supreme Court, Judge Burton Roberts. As a result of the screening at the Bronx County courthouse, I received invitations to assist in drafting legislation amending New York's drug laws to give courts discretion in sentencing drug mules.

In 1993, New York State Assembly Codes Committee Chair Joseph Lentol introduced the amending legislation. He held hearings on the Rockefeller Drug Laws to solicit the views of criminal justice professionals across the state about the 'drug mule bill' and additional proposed changes in the drug laws.

Testimony by prosecutors, judges, law enforcement and corrections officials, defence attorneys, and drug policy analysts again revealed a consensus within the New York criminal justice community that drug mules play only marginal roles in the drug trade; that such roles preclude mules from benefiting from the laws' provision for lifetime probation in exchange for material assistance; and that harsh mandatory prison terms required by law for drug mules neither reduce drug traffic nor deter others from acting as mules.[15]

Despite this consensus, the drug mule bill has yet to be enacted in New York – a casualty, it seems, of 'tough-on-crime' politics.

As public and policy maker interest in the predicament of the drug mules grew, Sister Marion herself became the subject of media profiles. Word about the pugnacious nun spread throughout New York's criminal justice community. Doors previously closed to her and her charges began to open.

Today, Sister Marion regularly shares information about individual cases with senior staff at the Queen's district attorney's office, who now promptly return her phone calls. She frequently accompanies women defendants to court and writes letters on their behalf to increasingly responsive judges. She performs an invaluable service in a place like New York City, where a system deluged with drug cases prevents probation workers or public defenders from gathering background information that may be crucial to prosecutorial and judicial decision-making. Even the local public defenders, with whom she often wrangled in the early years of her crusade, now afford the good sister grudging respect for her success in obtaining better outcomes in many cases than they would have achieved on their own.

Notwithstanding the importance of such individual efforts to change policy at the local level, women continue to come in droves through JFK to Riker's. As of this writing, there has been an enormous increase in the number of women travelling from Jamaica, where Colombian drug lords have established a major new trans-shipment point for cocaine destined for the United States. It is obvious that the poor or unfortunate women of Jamaica have become yet another source of cheap and expendable labour in the deal.

Turning the corner

Beneath the din of tough-on-crime shouting in the White House and Congress, a quiet strain of sober reason has begun to emerge in the fight against drugs.

So stated a recent *New York Times* editorial regarding agreement between the House and Senate to eliminate federal mandatory minimum sentences for certain low-level drug offenders, 'the mules and messengers of drug operations'.[16] Even though this historic consensus is buried in a federal crime bill chockful of enhanced penalties, it is clear that Congress has turned a major conceptual corner in the war on drugs.

The impetus for change has been building for some time. US policy makers have been convinced of the need for change by media coverage of horror stories such as the ones I have described; by judges leaving the bench or refusing to try drug cases because of the harsh sentences imposed on drug mules and other low-level drug offenders; and by federal and state prosecutors fashioning approaches to plea bargaining that now routinely 'bump down' charges against accused drug mules. By mid 1993, key members of Congress had begun to talk publicly about their potential support for a 'safety valve' for low-level drug offenders facing mandatory sentences under federal law.

The turning point, however, came in the form of a US Department of Justice (DOJ) study, completed in the summer of 1993 but withheld from the public until February 1994. This study found that of the 90,000 federal prison inmates, one-fifth (21.1 percent) were low-level drug offenders, defined as 'non-violent offenders with minimal or no prior criminal history whose offence did not involve sophisticated criminal activity and who otherwise did not present negative characteristics which would preclude consideration for sentence modification'.[17] Of these low-level drug offenders, almost half were drug couriers or played peripheral roles in drug trafficking, and two-thirds had received mandatory minimum sentences. The key determinant of their sentences was the quantity of drugs involved. Culpability had only a small influence on the length of the sentence. Furthermore, the study found no significant difference between sentences given to drug defendants with minor functional roles (eg. drug mules) and defendants who played much more significant roles in a drug scheme (eg. drug lords).

The study revealed that federal drug offenders, even those with minor or no past criminal behaviour, are receiving much longer sentences than they were prior to the 1986 Anti-Drug Abuse Act, which established most of the mandatory minimum penalties for drug trafficking and importation. In many cases, defendants are receiving a prison sentence when previously they would have received probation. Finally, the study concluded that low-level drug law violators are much less likely than high-level defendants to reoffend after their release from prison and, if they do reoffend, they are unlikely to commit a crime of violence.

The importance of the DOJ study to the debate over sentencing policies for drug offenders lies primarily in its careful research on the functional role in the drug trade played by offenders who are subject to these policies and in its strong implication that reliance on drug quantities as the primary determinant of the nature and length of punishment produces unfair and unreasonable results. Because drug quantities are the linchpin of state and federal drug policies, drug policy planners and practitioners at all levels would do well to study the results of this research.

For those interested in the impact of US drug sentencing policies on women and foreign nationals, the DOJ study contains the first analysis available on the gender, citizenship, and functional role of drug offenders imprisoned in the United States. This analysis shows that the most distinctive difference between low-level and high-level drug offenders is that the *low-level group is disproportionately female and foreign.*

These findings confirm the contention that women drug couriers and their treatment by our criminal justice system deserve special scrutiny. Recently, legal scholars and criminologists have begun to advance the notion that 'gender-blind' sentencing models are disadvantageous for women, in part because they do not allow for consideration of the minor roles that women tend to play in many offences.[18] The irony is, of course, that this has been difficult to prove given the paucity of research on offender culpability and the lack of gender-specific data.

The Justice Department study also underscores the need for US criminal justice policy makers and practitioners to consider the problem of drug couriers within a global context. We cannot afford to ignore the evidence pointing to increasing involvement in the drug trade by the governments and military forces of struggling and fledgling nations. We cannot afford to turn away from the fact that such involvement portends continued and even increased use of vulnerable and desperate populations as a source of cheap, expendable courier labour. Finally, we should face squarely the likelihood that our drug-war strategies, adopted by many other nations, have so far resulted only in the re-victimization of many people already suffering under grinding poverty and corrupt political regimes.[19]

Policy makers and practitioners must do more to link such evidence to law-enforcement and sentencing policies and practices as they pertain to drug couriers. I often wonder whether things could have gone differently for Sonia, the drug mule living with two young children in Miami, who suffered a permanent 'psychotic break' while detained in a New York jail on charges of drug importation. Would information about Haitian officials' involvement in drug trafficking – information that is now front-page news – have made her story of coercion in Haiti more believable to the authorities? Would use of such information by legislators, defenders, prosecutors, judges, or immigration authorities have allowed somebody to offer this mother something other than a Solomon's choice between lengthy imprisonment and deportation?

For Sonia, it is too late. But there is time to consider these arguments for the many other women like Sonia who are the conscripts and prisoners of a drug war the United States has shipped around the World.

Notes

1. An earlier version of this article appeared in *Criminal Justice*, Winter 1995, Volume 9, Number 4.
2. Tracy Huling, *Women Drug Couriers: What Do We Know and What Does It Mean?* The Faces of Change: Policy Track Manual for the Seventh International Conference on Drug Policy Reform, Drug Policy Foundation, 1993.
3. Rosa del Olmo, *The Economic Crisis and the Criminalisation of Latin American Women*, 17 *Soc.Just.* 40 (1990).
4. Ayesha Tarzi and John Hedge, *A Prison Within a Prison: A Study of Foreign Prisoners*, Inner London Probation Service, 1990, App. 4.
5. Penny Green, *Drug Couriers*, Howard League for Penal Reform, 1991, p. 13.
6. Rosemary Abernethy and Nick Hammond, *Drug Couriers: A Role for the Probation Service*, Middlesex Area Probation Service, 1992, p. 36.
7. John van Putten, *Drug couriers: Offenders or Victims in the War on Drugs?*, Report on the Two days Bilateral Seminar, Nederlandse Federatie Van Reclasseringsinstellingen, 1993, p. 16.
8. Green, op. cit., p. 13.
9. del Olmo, op. cit., p. 40.
10. Margaret Shaw, *Paying the Price: Federally-Sentenced Women in Context*, Corrections Branch, Ministry of the Solicitor General of Canada, Ottawa, 1991, pp. 20–21.
11. Tracy Huling, *Injustice Will Be Done: Women Drug Couriers and the Rockefeller Drug Laws*, Correctional Association of New York, 1992.
12. A total of twenty-eight years for the group as a whole.
13. Indeed, arrests of women declined during this period in Manhattan, the Bronx, and Staten Island.
14. For more discussion of this point, see Myrna S. Raeder, *Gender Issues in the Federal Sentencing Guidelines and Mandatory Minimum Sentences*, 8(3) *Crim. Just.* 21, 60–62 (Fall 1993).
15. Transcripts, New York State Assembly Standing Committee on Codes, *Public Hearing: The Rockefeller Drug Laws – 20 Years Later*, June 1993.
16. *Smarter, and Fairer, about Drug Crime*, New York Times, 26 June 1994.
17. Department of Justice (DOJ), *An Analysis of Non-Violent Drug Offenders with Minimal Criminal Histories*, 1994.
18. See Myrna S. Raeder, *Gender and Sentencing: Single Moms, Battered Women, and Other Sex-Based Anomalies in the Gender-Free World of the Federal Sentencing Guidelines*, 20(3) *Pepperdine L. Rev.* 905 (1993); Kathleen Daly, *Gender, Crime and Punishment*, Yale University Press, 1994.
19. See Ethan Nadelmann, *Cops Across Borders: The Internationalisation of US Criminal Law Enforcement*, Pennsylvania State University Press, 1993.

5
Drug Couriers: The Response of the German Criminal Justice System

Hans-Jörg Albrecht

Introduction

Drug couriers play an essential role in the drug market but have been largely ignored within German criminology. Even though most illicitly-used drugs are imported into Germany (with the exception of some amphetamines, LSD and pharmaceutical drugs), there is not even a clear definition of a drug courier.

However, interest has been shown by the police and customs agencies who have developed drug interdiction schemes while general surveys and clinical samples have focused on drug users and addicts.

The criminal courts have produced an extensive body of decisions relating to couriers and there have been significant developments in legal theory, especially in relation to the doctrine of complicity.[1]

The policing focus on borders has stimulated the development of special investigative techniques designed to identify the profiles of drug couriers whose activities have also been a subject of the debate on the abolition of border controls generated by the Schengen agreement.[2]

At the same time, the image of the drug courier or drug trafficker has been linked with foreign nationals and ethnic minorities. The topic 'ethnicity and drug trafficking' is politically sensitive and has been exploited by the new right wing parties and extremist groups who argue that ethnic minorities, in particular, asylum seekers, are a threat to public safety.[3]

A recent analysis of the content of Germany's print media reveals that two fifths of articles relating to foreigners highlighted the topic of 'crimes committed by foreign minorities'.[4] Sixty percent of these articles highlighted drug trafficking and organised crime.[5]

Overall, ethnic minorities and drug traffickers are being increasingly linked in a manner which hinders independent analysis of either phenomenon.[6]

Overview of the legislative framework

1. The history of German drug laws

The origins of German criminal legislation in the field of psychoactive and other drugs dates back to the first decades of the 20th century.[7] In 1929, the Act on Opium and Opium Derivatives, the so-called 'Opium Law', represented the first legislative effort to bring drugs under the control of administrative and criminal law. This Act largely remained intact until the 1960s when a wider debate on drug policies, centred around the issue of cannabis, began.

This debate led to the 1971 Act on Narcotics (Betäubungsmittelgesetz) which supplanted the 1929 Act and, in response to the arrival of heroin on the German drug scene in the late 1970s, was amended in 1981 by the 'Heroin Law' (Act on Narcotics of 28 July 1981, Bundesgesetzblatt).[8]

The 'Heroin Law' made an important distinction between drug users and drug traffickers. When the emphasis had been on cannabis, trafficking and use were treated together and German nationals constituted the majority of offenders.

In the 1980s, legislative efforts turned to the problem of organised, large-scale drug trafficking. In the Federal Republic of Germany, this led to wider attempts to cope with organised crime and illegal profits and to improve the investigation of 'victimless' drug crime. The Law on Drug Trafficking and Other Types of Organised Crime was passed on 15 July 1992.

2. The development of drug laws

There are a number of trends underpinning the development of drug laws in the Federal Republic of Germany.

Maximum penalties for drug offences have increased: serious narcotics offences now carry a maximum of 15 years imprisonment, the longest sentence available except for life imprisonment. Offences covering courier activities, especially the importation and sale of drugs, rank amongst the most serious drug offences. 'Attempted offences' have been upgraded to independent offences and the range of drugs falling within the Narcotics Act has been expanded.

Illicit drugs are not explicitly defined in the Narcotics Act. Instead, reference is made to a list of drugs in the annex which may be extended or amended without recourse to Parliament. The annex divides illicit drugs into three groups: drugs which may be prescribed by physicians; drugs which cannot be prescribed but may be used and trafficked for other purposes; and drugs which may not be prescribed, possessed or trafficked for any reason.

Of the commonly used drugs, cocaine and amphetamine are listed as narcotics which may be prescribed for certain specified purposes. Heroin and cannabis, the most widely distributed illicit drugs, cannot be trafficked or prescribed.

As mentioned above, the 1981 amendment to the Law on Narcotics aims to distinguish drug addicts from non-addicted traffickers and dealers. It provides for the dismissal of criminal cases or the postponement of prison sentences for addicts if the sentence does not exceed two years and the offender agrees to be treated in a licensed treatment unit.

Different models for controlling the supply of drugs and the demand for drugs have thus been adopted: while rehabilitative goals guide the control of demand, deterrence through severe sentencing is presented as an efficient means of controlling supply as part of a general response to organised crime.

During the 1970s and early 1980s, the medical profession had a marginal role (through very restrictive regulations on prescriptions) in the approach to drug control. However, since the mid 1980s, partly because the spread of Aids is associated with intravenous drug use, the medical profession has played a more direct role, especially through the development of methadone programmes.

3. The general policy towards drug markets

German public policy has always focused on the supply side of the drug market. This is reflected by the extended penalties for importation, trafficking and trading, especially in large quantities. Interdiction of drugs at the borders and the elimination of drug distribution networks are among the most prominent goals of drug law enforcement.[9] Increased co-operation is being sought from law enforcement agencies in drug-producing and exporting countries.

This policy is justified by the assumption that a reduction in the availability of illicit drugs will keep the domestic price high and therefore discourage traffickers.

The policy aimed at the drug user and the demand side of the market reflects ambivalent attitudes towards drug use and addiction. Although the German criminal justice system has historically been bound by the principle that self-injuries or mere immoral behaviour should not be regarded as criminal acts (ie. personal drug use should not be a criminal offence), drug users are explicitly targeted by the criminal law, largely because it is impossible for a user to consume drugs without first committing the criminal offence(s) of possession and/or purchase.

The extension of the criminal law to cover the user is justified by the argument that black markets depend on demand and that targeting the demand will ultimately reduce the supply. Despite such arguments, the Constitutional Court ruled on 9 March 1994 that importation, possession and purchase of minor quantities of drugs solely for personal use must be exempted from punishment, as punishment would violate the principle of proportionality.[10]

4. Drug offences

'Ordinary' drug offences are defined in section 29 I of the Act on Narcotics to encompass production, trafficking, importing, exporting, acquiring, selling, possession, transit, purchase, advertising, financing drug trafficking, trafficking and commerce in narcotics, public announcement of opportunities to purchase or consume drugs, illegal prescription of controlled drugs by physicians or illegal supply by pharmacists. Trafficking in 'look-alikes' or selling and supplying fake drugs is also an offence under section 25 VI of the Act.

Penalties include imprisonment for up to 5 years or a fine (of 5 to 360 units), although ordinary offences may be exempted from punishment if minor amounts only are involved and were intended for personal use (section 31a). Although the wording of section 31a refers to discretionary powers, the decision of the Constitutional Court cited above (see footnote 10) obliges the Public Prosecutor to dismiss a case for importation, purchase and possession if a minor amount for personal or occasional use is involved.

Under section 29a, the minimum penalty is increased to 1 year imprisonment, and the maximum to 15 years, if a person aged 21 or more procures drugs for a minor of 18 years or less; if a person aged 21 or more seduces a minor into trafficking illicit drugs; or if a person produces, possesses, procures or trafficks a 'non-minor amount' of drugs.

The Superior Courts have defined what constitutes a 'considerable', 'normal' or 'minor' quantity of drugs.

The following quantities are considered 'considerable' and carry a minimum penalty of 1 year imprisonment: 7.5 grams of cannabis (tetrahydrocanabinol); 1.5 grams of heroin (hydrochlorid); 5 grams of cocaine (hydrochlorid); and 10 grams of pure amphetamine. These limits mean that drug couriers involved in importation regularly risk prison sentences under felony drug statutes.

'Minor' quantities include 0.15 grams of heroin, 300 micrograms of cocaine and up to 6 grams of hashish. For such amounts, section 31a of the Act on Narcotics allows for exemption from punishment, or requires it, if the criteria of the above Constitutional Court ruling are met.

Section 30 of the Act on Narcotics raises the minimum penalty to 2 years imprisonment if the offender is a member of a criminal enterprise; is trafficking in drugs professionally; procures drugs which result in the death of the user; or imports a 'considerable' amount of drugs.

In 1992, the minimum sentence was raised to 5 years imprisonment in cases where a 'considerable' amount of drugs is produced, trafficked, imported or exported and if the offender is a member of a continuing criminal enterprise specialising in drug trafficking.

5. Procedural aspects of drug law enforcement
The Act on Narcotics allows a drug offender to be used as a Crown witness and for other methods of investigation which undermine

the principle of legality prevailing within German criminal law procedure.

Crown witnesses may receive a more lenient sentence, or avoid punishment altogether, if the information supplied enables police or the Public Prosecutor to clear up other drug offences. Section 31 of the Law on Narcotics also allows wire-tapping, mail surveillance, the use of informants and undercover agents (the so-called 'verdeckte Ermittler' – covert investigator), 'buy and bust' operations and controlled delivery in the investigation of drug offences.[11]

Specific provisions in the procedural laws covering a range of criminal offences also apply to the investigation of drug offences.

Subject to conditions, section 100a no. 4 of the Criminal Procedural Code allows the use of wire-tapping in the investigation of serious offences while section 99 of the same Code allows the surveillance and seizure of mail during the investigation of any criminal offence.

Section 104 of the Criminal Procedure Code removes the restrictions on the search of premises at night if the premises are known as venues for drug trafficking.

Section 112a of the Criminal Procedure Code allows pre-trial detention on the additional ground that there are reasons to believe the suspect will continue to engage in serious drug offences.

The recently enacted Law on Organised Drug Trafficking and Other Types of Organised Crime contained statutes explicitly allowing the use of undercover agents (a restricted version of the 'verdeckte Ermittler') and the use of various technical devices in the investigation of serious organised crime. Although there are still some restrictions on the use of 'bugs' in apartments and premises, state laws governing police powers were amended during the 1980s to allow the wide use of techniques normally restricted to the secret services.

As a result of these developments, the distinction between preventative police tasks and repressive police tasks has been blurred.

General trends in drug law enforcement

1. The increasing number of drug offenders

The number of drug suspects recorded in police statistics rose from less than 1,000 in the 1960s to over 50,000 in the 1980s, and to over 90,000 at the beginning of the 1990s. In the early part of the 1960s, approximately 100 people per year were sentenced under the Opium Law. By the mid-1980s, almost 20,000 were being sentenced under the Act on Narcotics. In 1991, the number of adjudicated and sentenced drug offenders reached almost 28,000.[12]

The effects of this trend can be observed within the prison system. In the 1960s, drug offenders were virtually non-existent inside German correctional facilities. By the 1980s, every tenth prisoner had been sentenced for violating the drug laws.[13] Much of the overcorwding in the prison system in the 1980s was due to the sharp increase in long prison sentences meted out in serious drug cases.

In 1976, 10 percent of prison sentences of two years or more were for drug related offences. By 1991, the proportion had risen to 27 percent.[14] Until recently, these offences involved cannabis rather than hard drugs. In 1986, two thirds of all drug offences related to cannabis. By 1992, this had declined to 40 percent.

2. The preoccupation with small quantities

Most offenders are convicted or arrested for possession. Police data indicates that law enforcers are preoccupied with small amounts of drugs and that most of the offenders going through the criminal justice system are drug users. The Federal Government report on the implementation of the Narcotics Law for the period 1985–1987 shows that 80 percent of all criminal investigations concerned small amounts of drugs for personal use.[15]

A new analysis of drug enforcement data for the period 1988–1990 confirms this trend.[16] It looks at 90,000 final decisions of drug investigations and finds that although many cases are dismissed under sections 153 and 153a of the Criminal Procedural Code, out of 65,000 court decisions, 12,000 are for possession of less than 5 grams of cannabis and a further 12,000 for quantities of less than 50 grams. Therefore, almost 40 percent of drug related sentences are for minor amounts of soft drugs.

In the mid 1980s, one third of prisoners serving sentences for drug related offences in the state of Hessen were addicts. Approximately half of convicted couriers were trafficking less than 500 grams of any drug and while cocaine couriers are likely to receive lengthy sentences, the bulk of imprisoned drug offenders are either addicts or involved in low level trafficking.[17]

The changing characteristics of drug couriers

1. The growth of organised trafficking and importation

The individual trafficker, or small scale entrepreneur, was prevalent in the 1960s when there was little in the way of an organised market and cannabis was the most widely used drug.

During the 1970s and 1980s, trafficking and importation became highly organised and based in the drug producing and transit countries. This in turn lead to important changes in the ethnic backgrounds of couriers (see graphs 1 and 2 below).

These changes coincided with changes in the demand for drugs and in the nature of drug law enforcement. As drug control systems grew in size and efficiency, so did the market for heroin and cocaine. This coincided with changes in the movement of labour from drug producing countries. Those arrested as couriers increasingly come from India, Afghanistan, Pakistan, Iran, Africa and South America. These couriers typically are used solely as a means of transportation and are not involved in the organisation of drug trafficking or distribution.

Apart from the courier activities linking the drug producing countries and Germany, smaller distribution networks operate on a European, national and regional level. The levels of organisation within these networks vary enormously. There have been reports of well organised Kurdish 'families' involved in heroin trafficking and distribution and of Moroccan and Algerian groups dealing with cannabis. Less organised small-scale cross border trafficking at the Dutch German border involves individuals from the local scenes on an irregular basis. This corresponds with patterns of courier activity within Germany which are determined by variations in the price and availability of drugs.

2. The impact of law enforcement

Although law enforcement does not appear to affect the nature of drug trafficking in general, it is clear that the interaction between drug enforcement and courier activities does force steady changes in trafficking routes and adjustments to the way trafficking is organised. The dynamics of this interaction can be observed in relation to drug couriers. Police data from the state of Hessen differentiates several sub-groups of foreign minorities. In the early 1980s, Senegalese and Gambian offenders were almost exclusively associated with drug offences and were involved in heroin distribution in some metropolitan centres, especially in Frankfurt. During the second half of the 1980s, Senegalese and Gambian nationals faded out of police statistics, suggesting that police pressure had forced a dislocation in the methods of drug distribution.

Similar differentiations can be observed in the types of drug being carried by couriers. For example, German nationals constitute the majority of cannabis couriers, whereas foreign nationals predominate in the importation of heroin and cocaine (see graph 2 below). In 1991, foreign nationals constituted 94 percent of those convicted of cocaine importation in Frankfurt.[18]

According to police sources, most cannabis and heroin is smuggled in large quantities by land, while cocaine trafficking combines large and small quantities, often in an individual's luggage. The 'body packer' (ie. someone who swallows the drugs) is particularly associated with the trafficking of cocaine, although this is by no means an exclusive method of transporting the drug. Of the 96 individuals who were arrested for cocaine trafficking in 1987, 40 percent carried the drug on their person while the rest concealed the drugs in their luggage. Half of those who carried the drug on them were 'body packers'.[19]

3. Basic profiles

A breakdown of the 96 suspects shows that 75 percent were Colombians; 76 percent were male; and the mean age was 32, although ages ranged from 13 to 72. These couriers had received surprisingly high levels of education. One third had completed high school and a further 17 percent had been to university. Only 4 percent claimed to be unemployed but 80 percent gave financial problems or poverty as the motive for acting as a courier. These couriers took considerable risks. On average, they carried 636 grams with an average purity of 87 percent. This made them candidates for the felony drug offence statutes which carry minimum prison sentences of 1 or 2 years. Despite this, 86 percent confessed to the alleged drug offence.[20]

'Body packing' is also used for the importation of heroin. As Nigeria became a major port of transit during the late 1980s, increasing numbers of Nigerians, Senegalese and Gambians were arrested for this type of heroin transportation, reflecting their growing role in courier and small scale distribution activity.[21]

The trafficking of women and drugs has also merged in recent years. For example, Colombian prostitutes are often used as couriers before being transferred to red-light districts, where they become further enmeshed in cocaine distribution networks.[22]

The response of the criminal justice system

1. Strategies for identifying drug couriers

As discussed above, enforcement strategies have concentrated on drug supply interdiction. These strategies are partially reliant upon the official perceptions of drug couriers developed in recent years, when there has been an increasing exchange of intelligence between port-based customs liaison officers and police and customs officers involved in controlled delivery ('sting') operations.

Customs officers have also profiled the typical courier according to criteria such as age, length of journey, the route taken and the type and size of luggage. Incoming passengers matching these profiles may be subjected to physical examination within the terms of section 81a of the German Criminal Procedural Code. Between 1987 and 1989 inclusive, 1100 urine tests were conducted at Frankfurt airport, of which 220 proved positive. Physical examinations, including the use of x-rays, were undertaken on 645 people of whom 86 showed signs of carrying drugs in the body.[23]

2. Arrest and pre-trial detention

Although there is no specific data on the pre-trial detention of foreign drug couriers, statistics from the city of Frankfurt suggest that it is very common, especially for African and South American nationals. For example, in 1990, the ratio of suspects held in police custody followed by a police application for pre-trial detention to suspects avoiding preliminary deprivation of liberty was 1:1 for German nationals; 3:1 for Moroccans and Algerians; 4:1 for South Americans; 6:1 for Yugoslavs and Turks; and 7:1 for black Africans.[24] The study of cocaine couriers cited above found that pre-trial detention was used for nearly all suspected cocaine couriers and that the mean detention time was 9 months.[25]

From this we can tentatively conclude that pre-trial detention operates as an extra-legal means of punishment and deterrence.

3. Sentencing the courier

Research on sentencing is limited to cocaine couriers, virtually all of whom are sentenced for felony counts of importing 'non minor' (considerable) amounts. The penalties range from 2 to 15 years imprisonment[26] with the average sentence being 2 to 3 years.[27] It is important to note that within sentencing doctrine, couriers are regarded as accomplices to those who have organised the scheme of transport.[28]

The same research suggests that despite the inevitable severe penalties, 'guilty pleas' prevail, even though technically these are not available. No witnesses appeared in 10 percent of trials, no moves for new evidence were made in approximately 50 percent, appeals were rare, and more importantly, the average length of each trial was 3 to 5 hours.[29]

Little is known of the sentencing patterns for other sub-groups of couriers. However, sentencing of drug offenders is generally based on the type of drug and the amount involved.

4. Criminal corrections and drug couriers

a. Prison regimes

German criminal law limits the suspension of custodial sentences to those of less than 2 years duration. This effectively excludes drug couriers and necessitates an investigation of the type of prison regime which operates for them.

A general prison survey in the state of Hessen shows that foreigners participate less in furlough and work release programmes.[30] As a proportion of those participating in furlough programmes, prisoners from Turkey and other European countries rank second behind German nationals but are ahead of prisoners from South

America, Africa and the Middle East. South American and African prisoners suffer extreme isolation. They tend to be serving long sentences for courier activities, have no relationship to the country in which they are sentenced and, unlike the Turks, no access to a local ethnic minority community.

b. Parole and deportation

Under section 456a of the German Procedural Code, foreign nationals sentenced to imprisonment can be released after half the sentence is served on the condition that they are deported immediately. If this does not apply, parole normally is granted after two thirds of the sentence has been served. The available data suggests that drug couriers usually are paroled and deported to their home country some 3 to 4 months before two thirds of the sentence is served.[31]

There is some reluctance to limit the time served to half the initial sentence although in recent years, some state governments have shown an interest in reducing the time foreign nationals spend in prison because of the potential reductions in the overall costs of criminal corrections.

Notes

1. See Kühne, H-H., Kriminalitätsbekkämpfung durch innereuropäische Grenzkontrollen? Auswirkungen der Schengener Abkommen auf die innere Sicherheit, Berlin 1991, p. 12.
2. See Körner, H-H., Betäubungsmittelgesetz Kommentar, 4th edition, München 1994, pp. 412, 416.
3. Walter, M. and Kubink, M., Ausländerkriminalität – Phänomen oder Phantom der (Kriminal-) Politik? Monatsschrift für Kriminologie und Strafrechtsreform 76 (1993), pp. 306–317.
4. Kubink, M., Verständnis und Bedeutung von Ausländerkriminalität. Eine Analyse der Konstitution sozialer Probleme, Centaurus, Pfaffenweiler 1993, p. 87.
5. ibid., p. 93.
6. Examples can be found in North America, where control of opiates in the 19th century is attributed to opium smoking by Chinese immigrant workers; and in England, where the National Drug Law Enforcement Unit has been established within the central Drugs and Illegal Immigration Unit. See Pearson G., Political Ideologies and Drug Policy, paper presented at the Third European Colloquium on Crime and Public Policy in Europe, Noordwijkerhout, 5–8 July 1992.
7. For a thorough review of the history of German drug laws, see Scheerer, S.,

Die Genese der Betäubungsmittelgesetze in der Bundesrepublik Deutschland und in der Niederlanden, Göttingen 1982.

8. Albrecht, H-J., Landesbericht Deutschland, in Meyre, J., (Hrsg.) Betäubungsmittelstrafrecht in Westeuropa, Freiburg 1987, S.63–168.
9. Nationaler Rauschgiftbekämpfungsplan, Bonn 1990.
10. Bundesverfassungsgericht Neue Juristiche Wochenschrift 1994, p. 1577; see also Kreuzer, A., Die Haschisch-Entscheidung des Bundesverfassungsgerichts, Neue Juristiche Wochenschrift, 1994, p. 2400.
11. See Albrecht, H-J. and van Kalmthout, A., eds., Drug Policies in Western Europe, Freiburg 1989.
12. Statistisches Bundesamt (Ed.), Strafverfolgung 1991, Wiesbaden 1994, p. 33.
13. Statistisches Bundesamt (Ed.), Rechtspflege, Reihe 4, Strafvollzug, Wiesbaden 1990, p. 32.
14. Statistisches Bundesamt (Ed.), Strafverfolgung, op. cit., p. 128.
15. Bericht der Bundesregierung über die Rechtsprechung nach den strafrechtlichen Vorschriften des Betaubungsmittelgesetzes in den Jahren 1985 bis 1987. Bundesstags-Drucksache 11/4329 vom 11.4.1989.
16. Bundestagsdrucksache 12/2838 of 17.6.92.
17. Albrecht, H-J., Voraussetzungen einer Entkriminalisierung im Drogenbereich, in Institut für Konfliktforschung (Hrsg.), Entkriminalisierung im Drogenbereich, Köln 1991, pp. 1–37.
18. Polizeipräsidium Frankfurt a.M., Polizeiliche Kriminalitätsstatistik 1991, Frankfurt 1992, p. 190 (N=184 suspects). Foreign nationals accounted for 78 percent of the heroin suspects; 56 percent of cannabis suspects came from other countries.
19. Körner, H-H., Der Schmuggel und der Handel mit Betaubungsmitteln in Körperöffnungen und im Körper, Strafverteidiger 1988, pp. 448–451.
20. Kraushaar, H., Der Korperschmuggel von Kokain, Frankfurt 1992, p. 52.
21. Kriminalabteilung Frankfurt a.M., Rauschgift-Lagebericht 1990, Frankfurt 1991, p. 54.
22. Polizeipräsidium Frankfurt, Polizeiliche Kriminalstatistik 1992, Frankfurt 1993, p. 10.
23. Kraushaar, H., Der Körperschmuggel von Kokain. Eine empirische Untersuchung zum illegalen Drogenimport unter besonderer Beachtung kriminologischer, kriminalistischer und strafprozessualer, Giessen 1992, p. 154.
24. Kriminalabteilung Frankfurt a.M., Rauschgift-Lagebericht 1990, Frankfurt 1991, pp. 4, 9.
25. Kraushaar, H., op. cit., p. 158.
26. ibid., p. 166.
27. ibid., p. 168.
28. Körner, H-H., Betäubungsmittelgesetz, Kommentar, 4th edition, München 1994, p. 412.
29. Kraushaar, H., op.cit., p. 166.
30. Albrecht, H-J., Ethnic Minorities, Crime and Public Policy, in R. Hood (Ed.), Crime and Criminal Policy in Europe, Oxford Centre for Criminological Research 1989, pp. 174–181.
31. Kraushaar, H., op. cit., pp. 275–276.

Graph 1
Suspects characteristics in case of import of non-minor amounts of drugs
1986-93

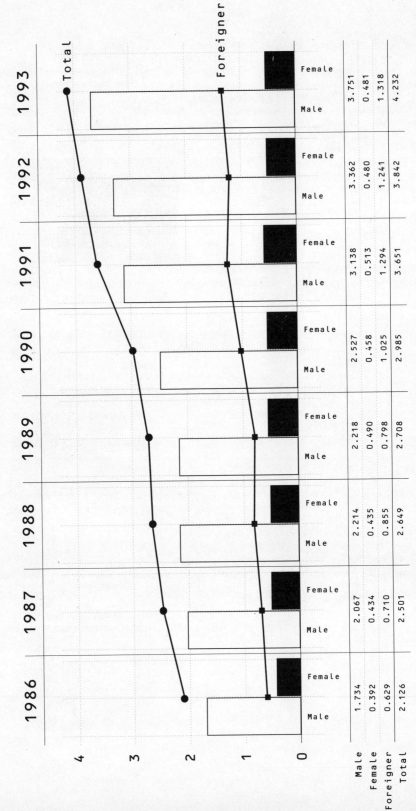

	1986	1987	1988	1989	1990	1991	1992	1993
Male	1.734	2.067	2.214	2.218	2.527	3.138	3.362	3.751
Female	0.392	0.434	0.435	0.490	0.458	0.513	0.480	0.481
Foreigner	0.629	0.710	0.855	0.798	1.025	1.294	1.241	1.318
Total	2.126	2.501	2.649	2.708	2.985	3.651	3.842	4.232

Graph 2

Importation of 'non-minor' amounts of drugs
Proportions of German and Foreign Nationals
1993 in %

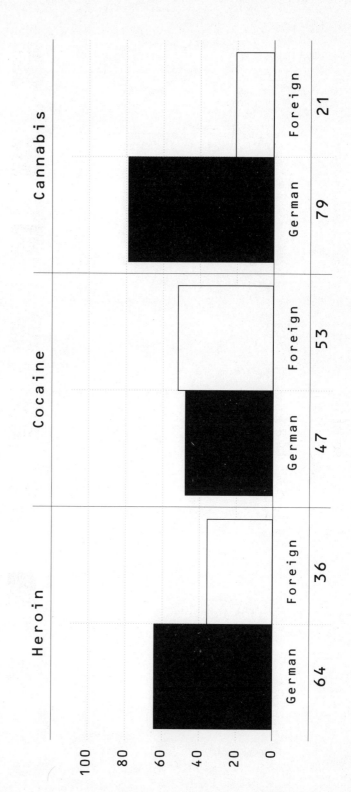

Source: Police Statistics 1993

II

Practitioner Analysis
and Research

1

The Sentencing of Drug Couriers

Rudi F. Fortson

Introduction

On the 22nd September 1995, a Recorder at Chelmsford Crown Court passed a sentence of 18 months' imprisonment on a male who pleaded guilty to the unlawful importation of one kilogram of cannabis resin (Class B) and 700 'squares' of lysergide (LSD: Class A). In the light of numerous sentencing decisions of the Court of Appeal, the overall sentence was compassionate if not lenient[1] and the Recorder appropriately took into account facts which typify many couriers who attract the label 'mules'. In this case the defendant (a British national) was intercepted at the port of Harwich having arrived by ferry from Holland. Strapped to his back was a package containing a block of cannabis resin to which was attached an envelope containing two cards impregnated with LSD. The defendant knew he was importing cannabis but denied knowledge of the LSD. That last fact afforded him no defence[2] but it was capable of amounting to some mitigation[3] and indeed the Recorder sentenced him on that basis. Although the defendant had a history of offending, none of his offences were drug related and he had a history of being used by others. As the Recorder remarked, organisers often do use 'stupid people' to run the risk of detection and to this list can be added the elderly, the disabled and persons who are socially disadvantaged.

Usually, couriers have no record of offending but the personal circumstances of the courier are unlikely to make a significant impact on sentence because deterrence, and not the reformation of the offender, is at the heart of the United Kingdom's sentencing strategy against drug-trafficking. In this regard, the United Kingdom does not stand alone and the usual justification for a harsh sentencing policy stems from the international nature of drug trafficking and the international response to combat it. Most of the popular drugs distributed on the illicit market in this country have to be imported and it is therefore the courier who occupies the front-line in any smuggling venture. In many cases, the courier may be able to provide law-enforcers with the information necessary to trace the source of supply and, for this reason, the courts have put 'assistance' to investigating officers high on the list of major mitigating factors which entitles the court to 'discount' the sentence imposed. On the other hand, it frequently happens that couriers are apprehended through surveillance techniques and intelligence reports, in circumstances where the line of supply is already established. In these cases, the courier is unlikely to be of much, or any, assistance to the authorities and the mere fact that a courier is *willing* to assist has far less clout as mitigation than valuable assistance actually given.

The principle of deterrence is thus tempered by discounts for any assistance provided by the offender so that the actual sentence imposed may have at least as much to do with pragmatism as endeavouring to make the punishment fit the crime. Whereas a plea of guilty may often be evidence of remorse, which justifies some discount on sentence, the same cannot be said in respect of assistance given which is likely to be motivated by self-interest. Some couriers talk freely believing that they can 'handle the situation' if news of their cooperation leaks out but many couriers, even if they did not act under duress, fear reprisals if they cooperate. However, their fear often amounts to little or no mitigation on the grounds that if the offence itself was not committed involuntarily (ie. under duress: which is a complete defence) the law will make no allowance for an offence committed for other personal reasons.

In this discussion, it would be idle to pretend that international pressure does not influence sentencing considerations where couriers are concerned. As we shall see, sentencing policy is linked with a series of conventions, treaties and agreements concerning both the creation of offences, and penalties, for drug offences – including simple possession. Developments on this front are supported by other international efforts to improve 'mutual assist-ance' and cooperation between law enforcement agencies.

The level of sentencing in respect of drug couriers is a matter for the domestic courts but when one country is seen to be out of line with the consensus of international opinion, pressure is brought to bear on it. Thus both in *The Times*[4] and the *Independent*[5], it is reported that the Dutch government proposes a more repressive regime in respect of the enforcement and punishment of drug offences. It proposes a 50 percent reduction in the number of coffee-shops which are permitted to distribute cannabis and to introduce compulsory detention for addicts who commit crimes which may not otherwise carry an automatic prison sen-tence. It is reported that in a recent poll, 75 percent of the Dutch regard present drug policies 'too lenient' and that international pressure has 'forced new curbs' on the use and distribution of drugs notwithstanding that the Netherlands has one of the lowest proportions of drug addicts in Europe.

There is no doubt that a considerable amount of Class A and Class B drugs is imported into the United Kingdom from the Netherlands. Clutterbuck[6] claims that the world 'is losing the war against drugs and Britain is no exception'. His assertion has been voiced by other commentators many times and is difficult to refute.

According to the Government's White Paper *'Tackling Drugs Together'* (1994, Cm 2678), at least 6 percent of the population of the United Kingdom take a controlled drug of some description and that among school children, 3 percent of 12 to 13 year olds and 14 percent of 14 to 15 year olds admit to consuming a controlled drug. These figures do not mean of course that there are three million addicts in this country nor does it follow that anything like this number will persistently and regularly take illegal sub-stances. By contrast a survey carried out by the BBC *'Drugwatch'* team, in 1986, suggested that at least four million people in Britain have *tried* drugs[7] but this figure now seems hopelessly out of date and is likely to be very much higher. Official statistics, provided by the law enforcement agencies, do not provide a true reflection of the pattern of drug distribution and use in this country. For example, the number of persons convicted, cautioned (or dealt with by compounding) for drug offences is minuscule and averaged some 47,000 persons per year during 1990 to 1992.[8] The gulf between actual offending and detection is therefore obvious.

Of the drugs consumed in this country, cannabis is the most popular. Twenty-four per cent of persons aged between 16 to 29 years report long term cannabis use but the 1990s have witnessed the introduction of Ecstasy into the drug culture and a revival of the use of LSD. Of those aged between 16 to 19 years, some 3 percent have tried LSD, 9 percent have tried Ecstasy and 11 percent have taken amphetamine. On the basis of information supplied to the author by drug users, LSD is often tried but seldom enjoyed and its use is not usually sustained, whereas Ecstasy produces an effect perceived as being much more pleasurable. What is frequently complained of are the number of pills passed off as Ecstasy but which are, in reality, a cocktail of undesired substances including LSD and Ketamine. Accordingly, figures, in relation to the consumption of LSD, may have something to say about what is being off-loaded by unscrupulous suppliers rather than what is actually wanted by the user. According to the Question Research and Marketing Strategists' Report (*Police Review*, March 1994),[9] of 80 offenders, aged between 15 and 24 years, 70 had tried cannabis, 26 had taken LSD (17 of whom are now regular users), 23 had tried heroin and 19 crack cocaine. Temazepam continues to pose a major social problem (when abused) which has resulted in further restrictions being imposed in respect of the possession and distribution of that substance.[10]

What is clear from all of this is that, despite the actions of Parliament and the courts, the scale of drug consumption and drug trafficking in this country is not diminishing but is becoming more extensive. According to Clutterbuck, Britain is second only to Italy in Western Europe in drug abuse in proportion to the population.[11] Worldwide, some $500 billion is expended on illicit drugs[12] and it has been suggested that £700 million was spent by persons attending 'raves' in the United Kingdom on Ecstasy during 1993.[13] Without commenting on whether this figure is likely to be correct, the fact remains that most of the drug is imported (approximately 1,162,015 doses were seized between 1990 and 1993) but, as with all cases of drugs imported, what is not clear is the amount of the drug which is destined for other countries. This is because the United Kingdom serves as a 'staging-post' in the distribution chain of controlled drugs between nations. Cocaine is exported directly from Colombia to the United States but one ruse is to ship the drug via the United Kingdom to the USA, Spain or other countries. Over the last 7 to 10 years, various African states have also emerged as distribution centres for the onward transmission of a variety of drugs to the USA, Western Europe and now, Eastern Europe and Russia.

The profile of the courier

Organisers of smuggling ventures are rarely successfully prosecuted before British courts. This is hardly surprising because the organiser will usually delegate risk-taking to others who are recruited for that purpose. Proving that a person was 'knowingly concerned' in a smuggling venture will often be relatively straightforward in respect of persons in possession of the drug (the courier or 'mule' being the classic example) but proving the requisite *mens rea* for a drug-related offence becomes more difficult in cases where the accused is shown to have a remote, or an apparently tenuous connection, with the offending venture. In the case of the courier, there will be varying degrees of knowledge. At one end of the scale, there will be couriers who will know the drug they are carrying, its value, purity and weight. Others may know that they are carrying a substance which they are forbidden to have in their possession or which is prohibited from importation but they do not know the nature of the prohibited substance they are carrying. Couriers often complain that they were misled as to the nature of the substance they were asked to carry (see *Bilinski (1988) 9 Cr. App. R.(S) 360* and see *Varshney* (1995) 16 Cr. App. R.(S) 267). As we shall see, this factor *may* afford some mitigation but it is not a defence.[14] It is unlikely that the courier will be told of the purity of the drug or what its street-value is likely to be. Clearly, where the courier is an innocent dupe – and they do exist – then no offence is committed according to the laws of the United Kingdom including a charge of 'possession' under section 5 of the Misuse of Drugs Act 1971 for the reasons given in *Warner v Metropolitan Police Commissioners* [1969] 2 AC 256.

Within the sentencing framework, advocates mitigating on behalf of the importer will look for two features that generally determine the parameters of sentencing: the 'primemover' or 'organiser' and the 'courier' or 'foot-soldier'.

To the advocate, the term 'courier' means more than just the person in possession of the drug and who brought about its import-ation. It is entirely descriptive and implies that the offender has the following characteristics:

i)   the person who shoulders all of the risk for the least reward (if successful) and carries the penalty for no reward (if unsuccessful);

ii) normally no history of offending;

iii) because a courier plays a subordinate role in the enterprise, that person's involvement may be explained at least, in part, by any external pressures or circumstances which persuaded the offender to become involved;

iv) the courier, having regard to the above, is likely to be genu-inely remorseful over their involvement in the offence; and

v)   the courier may not know precisely the nature, quality or value of the offending material which was in fact imported.

With that in mind, the nationality of the courier may be a relevant factor in mitigation if it helps to explain the circumstances in which the offender came to be involved and demonstrates the stress and anxiety which the offender will experience upon being imprisoned in a foreign country, separated from family and friends for what may be a considerable period of time.

Penny Green makes the point that no attempt had been made to determine a profile of the drug courier from an objective per-spective devoid of popular hype.[15] She concluded that drug couriers 'do not conform to the ungrounded imagery which vilifies them in the public mind' but that they represent 'a reality of Third World poverty and despair of men and women generally naive about drugs . . . whose offence was not motivated by greed but by familial concerns and economic desperation'. The contrary view is that couriers are motivated more by greed rather than by need but, as the authors of the Middlesex Area Probation Service report point out,[16] it is essential that each courier is assessed in the context of their own circumstances and that stereotypes should be avoided.

Couriers and nationality

Green *et al*[17] conclude that the majority of imprisoned illegal drug importers are from the developing world, particularly West Africa. Establishing how foreign nationals are punished, compared to British nationals, deserves thorough and proper investigation although it is not a task which can easily be performed given the lack of published official data that would be relevant for this purpose. On existing information it seems likely that most imprisoned importers are from countries of the developing world. Of course, some regard must be had to the fact that many of those countries are ideally placed, geographically speaking, for the production of popular controlled drugs. Thus, coca-leaf (cocaine) and cannabis naturally flourish in those countries which are seen as principal producers of those drugs. But this is by no means a complete answer because Nigeria, for example, is not a cocaine producer (although its climate may be suitable for growing the coca-leaf) and yet, as Clutterbuck points out,[18] it is now a major staging-post for the transmission of heroin and cocaine to Western Europe and the United States of America. Most Nigerian couriers are women but, irrespective of gender, the courier from this area is often poorly educated, in dire personal circumstances, who takes high risks for low reward.[19]

Green et al's research (based on three samples consisting of a total of 573 persons sentenced for drug importations through Heathrow and Gatwick Airports) found that most of the couriers of *cannabis* were of British nationality:

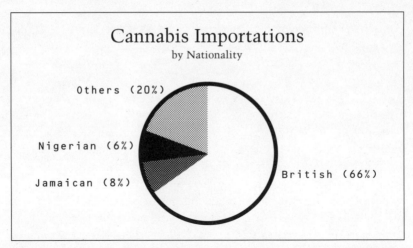

However, the results in respect of *cocaine* importations showed that a much lower percentage of British nationals acted as couriers although the value of the consignment relative to its weight was, of course, very much greater.

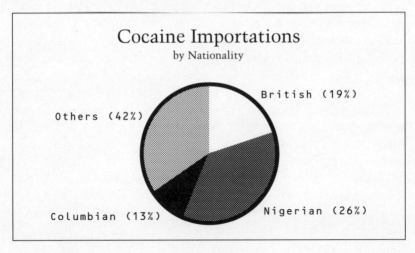

Again, only 17 per cent of British nationals were involved in the importation of *heroin*, compared to Nigerians who featured in 27 per cent of the cases:

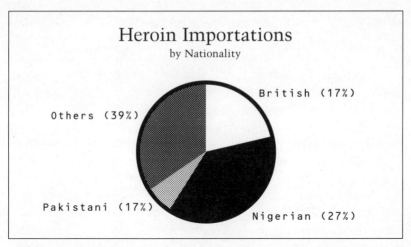

Heroin Importations
by Nationality

British (17%)
Others (39%)
Pakistani (17%)
Nigerian (27%)

Although on the results of this particular survey, the majority of cannabis importations involved a British national, few would accept that the research establishes a relationship between nationality and the type of drug imported or that there are differences in the ways in which people from different countries chose to import the drugs. Furthermore, on the basis of the information derived from Penny Green's study, it could be argued that British nationals were more likely to have swallowed cocaine or that the British nationals were more likely to be involved with lower value imports than Nigerians and Colombians. Such arguments would again not be accepted in many quarters as representing the true position. This is because the majority of substantial consignments of Class A and B drugs are imported by land and sea and not just by air. There is no accurate way of knowing how much is imported by *private* boats and aircraft. The use of Rigid Inflatable Boats (RIBs) seems to be increasing and this is because they are fast, rugged and their low profile makes detection difficult. Crews on small vessels are arguably couriers too even if they could not be labelled 'mules'.

Changing patterns

The patterns of importation and supply constantly change. This can be due to changes in demand and supply for different types of drugs and such patterns will also be significantly affected by operational or procedural changes introduced by airlines and other carriers. Political changes can have a dramatic impact on the structure of the distribution chain and also influence the way drugs may be imported. Nowhere has this been more apparent than in the case of Eastern Europe. Clutterbuck reports that Russia has some one million hectares under cannabis cultivation[20] and that street prices are very low. If true, it is not difficult to see how cannabis produced from that source is likely to find its way into the United Kingdom domestic market via a number of routes. Depending on the quality, the quantity of the harvest, the rate of detection of consignments imported into the United Kingdom, and the overall demand for cannabis, the emergence of Eastern European countries as producers of this drug could result in a new generation of couriers of an East European nationality.

Ecstasy is a Class A drug mainly manufactured in Holland and Poland. Many Dutch and British nationals are coming before the courts charged with the importation of the drug into this country, and there have been a number of cases involving British nationals exporting the drug to Spain or the Balearic Islands (eg. from Gatwick Airport). Although cannabis could be packaged and swallowed its bulk (in herbal or resin form), if brought by air and carried in, limits the smugglers' options as to how it can be imported in large quantities. During the 1970s and the early 1980s, the use of the 'two tartan-suitcase trick' was employed by couriers whether they were British nationals or not. The exportation of heroin from India to African countries by Africans who carried the drug in false bottomed suitcases is well known. Any survey, based on activities at only two airports, is not going to reveal indicators of general application to determine a proper profile of a courier. This is not the fault of researchers but a reflection of the lack of accurate data available to the public.

'Swallowers': motivations and limitations

The swallowing, of sometimes an incredible number, of packages of heroin or cocaine by the courier may be a rather more telling feature in favour of the courier. The risk to the life of the swallower, and the discomfort endured for very long periods of time, is obvious. So what drives a courier to do it? Many such couriers are persons without a criminal record whose personal circumstances may be dire, or unhappily their circumstances may be difficult to appreciate without the assistance of a carefully prepared and objectively written Pre-Sentence Report. No doubt there are swallowers who are motivated by greed and fuelled by a determination not to be apprehended, but most swallowers are driven to offending by external pressures of one sort or another.

To a sentencer, however, the issue is less clear cut. Desperation on the part of the courier (for example, to raise money to finance a life-saving operation for a relative back home) may be viewed by the sentencer as a selfish act when compared to the nature, quantity and quality of the drug which has been imported. But there is another, perhaps less obvious, reason why packages are swallowed. A swallower who arrives in the United Kingdom cannot be detained without charge forever. As the law once stood, a person suspected of carrying drugs internally could not be subjected to a medical examination, or to an X-ray, or be compelled to provide a sample of urine for the purposes of carrying out an 'Enzyme Multiply Immunoassary Technique' (E.M.I.T.) test without the suspect's consent. Without that consent, the officers had to hope that packages would be passed through the bowels by the suspect and collected in a special toilet facility before the time elapsed when the suspect had to be either charged, and brought before a court, or released. The swallowing of packages in strong plastic or rubber containers made the investigation of such cases more difficult and increased (in theory) the courier's prospects of being released if the demands of nature could be held back for long enough. A successful release of the suspect could also lead to the resumption of the venture to get the packages to the intended destination. However, it is difficult to gauge to what extent such exploits succeeded in practice. The demand for food and drink is difficult to resist and officers often display considerable skill in providing a suitable diet to obtain the desired evidence expeditiously. Of course, the person most likely to be aware of the finer points of law is the organiser and not the courier, whose concerns may be artificially allayed and who may be manipulated into believing that less risk attaches to the enterprise than is in fact the case.

Couriers as major players

Although sentencers distinguish between couriers and principals, difficulties arise when one moves away from the notion of a courier as a 'mule'. Clearly, some couriers do play more than just a subordinate role and might even be principal players in the smuggling operation. In *DPP v. Doot* (1972) 57 Cr. App. R. 600, five American nationals arrived in the United Kingdom in three vans, two of which contained cannabis resin totalling 129 kilograms. The drug had been concealed in wooden bases of sleeping beds specially constructed inside the vehicles by a carpenter in Belgium. The appellants collected the cannabis in Morocco and concealed it in the two offending vans. The plan was to ship the drug back to the United States. In one sense, the drivers of those vans could be described as 'couriers' but although Doot was 'the chief man', none of the appellants could appropriately be described as 'mules' and it does not seem that any of the appellants in that case sought to describe themselves as such. The courts will therefore often begin by ascertaining what is the 'appropriate' term of imprisonment, assuming no mitigation, having regard to the quantity and nature of the drug, and to then work down the gravity-scale to reflect mitigating factors.

In *Aranguren and others* (1994) 99 Cr. App. R. 347, the Lord Chief Justice said that: '. . . there are of course other important factors for the sentencing judge to consider such as the role played by the individual defendant, whether he has previously been convicted of drugs offences and, by way of mitigation, whether he has pleaded guilty or rendered assistance to the prosecuting authority'. Accordingly, the courts try and ascertain the position of the defendant in the smuggling team. This leads to the use of expressions which are intended to convey the reasons behind the sentence imposed even if, in fact, the expressions employed are not capable of precise definition. 'Courier' is one such a term and 'more than a courier' is another: see *Adewoye* (1988) 10 Cr. App. R.(S) 226; or 'a meeter': see *Aranguren* (1995) 16 Cr. App. R.(S) 211; or a 'minder': see *Arif* (1994) 15 Cr. App. R.(S) 895, and so on.

Domestic couriers

Most of the research undertaken on drug couriers focuses on those who transport drugs from one country to another. However, there is also a body of 'couriers' but who operate *domestically*. It is difficult to see why they should be excluded from the debate. Their role will often be as subordinate as in the case of their importing counterparts and for sentencing purposes, the distinction between a prime mover and a courier applies in the case of the person who acts as a 'driver' or even the 'minder' of a drug. The similarities are masked by the use of different charges.

In the case of importations of a controlled drug, a charge is usually brought under section 170(2) of the Customs and Excise Management Act 1979. The offence of being 'knowingly concerned' in the fraudulent evasion on the prohibition of a controlled drug (ie. prohibited by section 3 of the Misuse of Drugs Act 1971) is particularly widely drawn. The heart of the offence is the fraudulent *evasion* of the prohibition and it is therefore an error to construe the section as if it read 'fraudulent importation'. A person may commit an offence contrary to this section if they act before or even after the moment of importation. Thus, the person whose involvement only began after the drug was imported has no defence if the role played is to transport the consignment from one part of the country to another, knowing that the substance is one which must have been imported: see *Hussain* (1969) 52 Cr. App. R. 448; *Caiparra* (1988) 87 Cr. App. R. 316; *Ellis and Street* (1987) 84 Cr. App. R. 235. If the police are investigating the matter, they will seek to charge persons under the Misuse of Drugs Act 1971. Thus the courier who carried the drug into this country or who transports the drug within the United Kingdom would be charged by the police, not with the section 170(2) offence but with being in possession of a controlled drug with intent to supply (contrary to section 5(3) of the Misuse of Drugs Act 1971) or perhaps, if others are involved, with a conspiracy to contravene one of the provisions of the 1971 Act.

All 'couriers', by definition, do not intend to keep the drugs for themselves: they intend to supply it. The gravity of the offence is perhaps stated more graphically as an offence under s.5(3) of the 1971 Act (ie. possession with intent to supply). However, there may not be any significant difference in the result because the sentencing guidelines have introduced a degree of parity in respect of drug trafficking offences.

However, in *Fyffe* (1994) 15 Cr. App. R.(S) 13, the Court of Appeal reduced the sentence imposed on the appellant, who pleaded guilty to possessing 19 kilograms of cannabis resin with intent to supply it to another, from 4 years to 3 years imprisonment. The street value of the drug was said to be worth about £100,000. The appellant claimed he agreed to collect a package in Liverpool and to hand the drugs over to someone in Perth. Both the prosecution and the trial judge accepted that his role was that of a courier. Had the appellant been a 'courier' – in the context of an importation – there would have been no doubt that the *Aramah* guidelines would have applied[21] which stipulate 'importation of amounts up to about 20 kilograms of herbal cannabis or the equivalent in cannabis resin . . . will . . . attract sentences of between 18 months and three years . . .' The court of Appeal held that the sentence was outside the *Aramah* guidelines and reduced the sentence accordingly. So what influenced the original decision? The appellant's convictions were disregarded as being of no relevance and he had lost his job some months before the offence and 'was no doubt anxious to earn money by driving if he could'. The object lesson for sentencers is not to equate the courier with the wholesaler or retailer even though all three act within the chain of supply: and see *Morley* (1994) 15 Cr. App. R.(S) 86.

Including this type of courier in the debate may serve to explain how the relevant principles of law and sentencing practice are applied in practice in respect of the same or similar conduct.

The Sentencing guidelines

The courts no longer determine sentence by reference to the street-value of the drug because this was capable of leading to the paradox that if more of the drug was successfully imported over time, the lower the sentence might be if the street-value fell significantly (and vice versa).[22] Accordingly, where Class A drugs are involved and appear in powdered form, then where the weight of the drug (at 100 percent purity) was of the order of 500 grammes or more, sentences of 10 years and upwards may be imposed, but where the weight (again at 100 percent purity) is in the region of 5 kilograms or more, then sentences of 14 years to life imprisonment may be passed: *Aranguren and others* (1994) 99 Cr. App. R. 347.

Similar considerations apply when Ecstasy, which often appears in tablet form, is involved. The Court of Appeal heard evidence that, on average, a tablet contains 100mg. of the drug and therefore 5,000 tablets carry 10 years' imprisonment or more and 50,000 tablets carry 14 years' imprisonment and upwards: see *Warren and Beeley, The Times,* July 4, 1995. For LSD, see *Attorney-General's Reference Nos. 3, 4 and 5 of 1992* (1993) 14 Cr. App. R.(S) 191.

Guidelines for the importation of cannabis have always been expressed by reference to the weight of the drug: up to 20 kilograms of herbal cannabis (or the equivalent in cannabis resin or cannabis oil) will attract between 18 months' and three years' imprisonment; medium quantities over 20 kilograms will attract sentences between 3 to 6 years; and large scale importations will attract in the region of 10 years' imprisonment (*Aramah* (1982) 4 Cr. App. R.(S) 407).

Flexibility of sentence or mandatory terms?

Flexibility of sentencing is an inbuilt concept of the judicial process in the United Kingdom, notwithstanding the guidelines laid down by the Court of Appeal. Very few offences attract mandatory or fixed penalties; and even in cases of murder – which does attach a mandatory sentence (life imprisonment) – there have been repeated calls from eminent sources for a more flexible approach.[23] Although, in many countries, the sentencing of drug offenders is fettered by the application of mandatory penalties or requirements, any attempt to introduce this approach in the UK is likely be met with fierce resistance. We have therefore avoided *some* of the problems which are being experienced in countries which do apply much more rigid regimes.

For example, in the state of New York, offenders face a minimum of 15 years to life imprisonment for the possession of 4 ounces or more of a narcotic drug. Possession of two ounces of such a drug carries a minimum of 3 years. The personal circumstances of the offender are irrelevant and no allowance is made for a 'first-time' offence. Such an approach has been attacked by a number of commentators from within the American criminal justice community.[24] Tracy Huling reports that there is a 'consensus' that 'drug mules' play only marginal roles in the drug trade and that 'harsh mandatory prison terms required by law for drug mules neither reduce drug traffic nor deter others from acting as mules'.[25] She also points to a study, published in 1994, which found that of 90,000 federal prison inmates, 21.1 percent were 'low-level drug offenders' of whom almost half were drug couriers or who played peripheral roles in drug trafficking. Two-thirds had received mandatory minimum sentences yet they were persons with 'minimal or no prior criminal history whose offence did not involve sophisticated criminal activity and who otherwise did not present negative characteristics which would preclude consideration of sentence modification'.[26] Huling suggests that reliance on drug quantities, as the primary determinant of the nature and length of punishment, produces unfair and unreasonable results partly because culpability has only a marginal impact on the length of sentence and sometimes there is little difference between the terms imposed on couriers ('mules') and those who played a more significant role. There is force in this observation. Some couriers do feel that they might just as well be 'hanged for a sheep as a lamb'. This complaint is likely to be fuelled by the decision in *Aranguren* which demonstrates the problem. If 500 grams of pure heroin attracts between 10 to 14 years' imprisonment, while 5 kilograms of the drug attracts at least 14 years' imprisonment, is there not an incentive to import at least one kilogram for only a marginally higher stake?

Of course, advocates of the draconian regime argue that the question of whether the result is 'unfair or unreasonable' depends on whether the means is justified by the objective sought to be attained. They argue that severe sentences are designed to deter and that the amount actually imported is of secondary interest and that the initial stake must be a high one if it is to have any effect. The issue is whether couriers are the appropriate target for such a regime. Some research has been undertaken in the United States concerning the position and plight of drug 'mules', particularly in the case of women (see Huling, this volume). The metaphor of the 'mule' is not one which is generally heard in the United Kingdom to describe a drug courier and it *may be* that the reason for that lies in the fact that the label has emerged as a response to the sentencing policies as they are applied in the United States of America (albeit not consistently).

In 1993, hearings were held in New York with a view to amending the penal law in that State by way of a 'Drug Mule Bill'. The purpose of such a bill would be to empower the sentencer to impose a sentence on the 'mule' that is commensurate with the seriousness of the offence but which has regard to the personal circumstances and antecedents of the offender. To take this step would thus take them out of the front-line in the campaign against the trafficker. This might also have the effect of re-defining what is meant by a 'drug-trafficker' because, on this analysis, the courier or 'mule' is seen as being ancillary to that activity ie. a person whose task is menial and not in any way administrative or managerial in nature. Proponents of such a reform would presumably not accept that a 'special case' is being made for couriers but rather that their culpability should be viewed in isolation. The overriding difficulty is defining conduct which would permit this classification. An ingenious solution was proposed by the Correctional Association of New York who put forward the following draft:

(a) The defendant's conduct, for which the defendant was convicted, was limited to a single incident;

(b) The defendant's conduct was isolated from the criminal conduct of others, except insofar as another person solicited, requested, commanded, importuned or intentionally aided the defendant to receive, possess, transport and/or deliver the controlled substance, and the defendant did so;

(c) The defendant had no other participation or interest in or connection with any broader criminal transaction, conspiracy or enterprise to which the defendant's conduct related;

(d) Having regard to the nature and circumstances of the crime and to the history and character of the defendant, the court is of the opinion that the sentence otherwise required pursuant to subdivision two of section 60.05 of this article would be unduly harsh.

One difficulty with this draft is determining the circumstances in which it could properly be said that the defendant's conduct was truly 'isolated from the criminal conduct of others' notwithstanding the clarifying words which follow in (b) but which are perhaps made more ambiguous by (c). This is not a scenario in which the UK courts wish to become immersed and, in any event, it is a response to the harshness of a rigid sentencing regime as it is applied in the United States. It would be ideal to be able to say that such a proposal is unnecessary in our jurisdiction because sentencers enjoy generous latitude of discretion when sentencing drug offenders. This is not the perception of at least one commentator who has described the British scheme as 'essentially mandatory in nature' and that 'dismissal of mitigating factors sets the treatment of drug couriers apart from the treatment of most other offenders'.[27]

The development of English sentencing policy

Apart from notable exceptions, such as LSD and amphetamine sulphate, the most popularly consumed drugs in the United Kingdom have to be imported. This is also true of cannabis[28] and cannabis resin given that the home-grown product rarely matches the quality of the familiar products cultivated or produced overseas.

Parliament no doubt hoped, in 1971, that the enactment of the Misuse of Drugs Act would stem (if not eradicate) the rising tide of drug use. The scheme of the Act was to regulate the distribution and use of controlled drugs and to back up an administrative framework with an array of criminal offences. As originally drafted, the maximum term of imprisonment for certain drug trafficking offences in respect of a Class A or Class B drug was the same: 14 years. As the value of consignments of Class A drugs increased, sentences imposed for such offences became demonstrably out of step with penalties imposed by courts in foreign jurisdictions, with the complaint that Britain was a 'soft option' and thus a target for the shipment of drugs. As a result, the *Controlled Drugs (Penalties) Act 1985* increased the maximum term of imprisonment for a number of offences from 14 years' imprisonment (*in respect of a Class A drug*) to life imprisonment.

It could be argued that even by 1971, it was getting a little late to shut the stable-door. Much of the legislative response to drug consumption and drug trafficking is rooted in international obligations and treaties. The first significant development was the signing of the *International Opium Convention* at The Hague in 1912[29] which established the principle of international cooperation in the campaign against the trafficking in narcotics as a matter of international law. Two further conventions (held in Geneva in 1925[30] and 1931[31]) resulted in the setting up of the *Permanent Central Opium Board* and the *Drug Supervising Body*. Both of these bodies were replaced by the *International Narcotics Central Board* following the 'Vienna Convention' in 1961. The United Nations also plays a majr role in the development and implementation of international policies against drug trafficking.

The legislative approach in the United Kingdom has been necessarily piecemeal in response to changing domestic and international circumstances. The *Dangerous Drugs Act* 1920 (c.46) restricted the production, importation and exportation of opium and cocaine. That Act was amended by the *Dangerous Drugs Act 1925* (c.74) to restrict the importation and exportation of coca leaves as well as 'Indian hemp, and resins obtained from Indian hemp'.[32] Cannabis ('Indian hemp') was further controlled by the *Dangerous Drugs Act 1932* (c.15) which also amended the 1920 Act by restricting the importation, exportation, manufacture and sale of any 'extracts or tincture of Indian hemp' (section 8(1)) and this provision was extended to preparations of the same substance.[33] The Acts of 1920, 1925 and 1932 were consolidated, without amendment, by the *Dangerous Drugs Act 1951*. Following the *Single Convention on Narcotic Drugs 1961*, the Government enacted the *Dangerous Drugs Act 1964* (c.36) so as to be able to ratify the 1961 Single Convention. Accordingly, it became an offence for an occupier of premises to permit them to be used for the smoking of cannabis (section 9) and an offence to cultivate cannabis plants (section 10). The possession and importation of Lysergamide, and its derivatives, were restricted by the *Drugs (Prevention of Misuse) Act 1964* (c.64). The Dangerous Drugs Acts of 1951 and 1964 were consolidated by the *Dangerous Drugs Act 1965* (c.15) which, in turn, was repealed and replaced by the *Misuse of Drugs Act 1971* (c.38). That Act also repealed the Drugs (Prevention of Misuse) Act 1964.

Significantly, by Article 36 of the 1961 Single Convention,

member states are required to adopt measures which will ensure that 'cultivation, production, manufacture, extraction, preparation, possession, offering ... distribution ... importation and exportation of drugs ... shall be punishable offences when committed internationally, and that serious offences shall be liable to adequate punishment particularly by imprisonment ...'. Again, by Article 33, it was agreed that the parties 'shall not permit the possession of drugs except under legal authority'. The 1961 Convention has been ratified by a considerable number of states including the Netherlands.

As can be seen, unity of purpose has not been matched by a unity of approach between nations. Nevertheless, the approach of the United Kingdom government and courts has been to attack drug trafficking at the points of demand and supply.

Deterrent sentencing

For as long as the Court of Appeal (Criminal Division) has played its part in the formulation of sentencing policy and practice in respect of drug offenders, it has always been expressed that sentencing has a predominantly deterrent element to it.

Since 1982, the courts of first instance have sentenced mindful of the sentencing guidelines of the Court of Appeal in *Aramah* (1982) 4 Cr. App. R.(S) 407. However, long before the Misuse of Drugs Act 1971 fully came into force in 1973, the courts were declaring their intention to punish importers by the imposition of deterrent terms. For example, in *DPP v. Doot* (1972) 57 Cr. App. R. 600, five American nationals obtained three vans in Europe in which a carpenter in Belgium constructed beds with wooden bases. The vans were then taken to Morocco where 129 kilograms of cannabis were hidden in two of the vans and driven to this country where the appellants were arrested. The plan was to drive the vans to Liverpool and to ship them to Canada and down into the United States. There was evidence that Doot had succeeded in importing drugs in a similar fashion on an earlier occasion. The total value of drugs imported by Doot was said to be in the region of £90,000. This was in 1971/72. The street value today would be assessed at about £900,000 and yet Doot, who master-minded the whole operation, was sentenced to 33 months' imprisonment. He had pleaded guilty to the main charge after legal argument and was thus entitled to credit for that plea. Nevertheless, Lord Salmon took the opportunity to describe the sentences imposed as passing 'all understanding' and added that '. . . it hardly seems in accordance with the rules of international comity that our courts should treat [the defendants] with special leniency because their crimes were more likely to ruin young lives in the United States of America than in this country'. Significantly, he suggested that 'the minimum sentence normally imposed for unlawfully importing £30,000 worth of cannabis alone is certainly not less than 4 years' imprisonment for a defendant with a clean record'. At that time 60 kilograms of resin was worth at least £30,000.

In *Aramah* (1982) 4 Cr. App. R.(S) 407, the Court of Appeal upheld a sentence of 6 years imposed on an importer who smuggled 59 kilograms into the United Kingdom. It was his second such offence and the trial had been contested. In both cases the court endorsed the application of the deterrent principle when sentencing offenders engaged in the importation or supply of a controlled drug.

Sentencers, particularly during the 1970s and early 1980s, frequently prefaced their sentencing remark by saying that they were imposing a deterrent term 'so the message will go out' that the courts of this country will punish importers of a controlled drug 'severely'. This remark always did have a hollow, if not hopeless, ring about it. Many couriers, to whom such remarks have been addressed, were often too numb or too distressed to fully take on board what they had been told; some only partially understood what was said in court and needed to have the judge's remarks (and the sentence) explained; some felt too ashamed to tell their friends and family the truth, preferring to explain their absence on other grounds. Others maintained their innocence and no doubt continued to do so on their return home. Many couriers complain that they have been duped (totally or partially) and it is a complaint often made irrespective of gender. Others complain that they had been coerced into acting as they did. Others knew full well the risks they were taking but it was a calculated risk assessed against their own motives or personal difficulties. In such cases, the likelihood of *not* being apprehended is an important factor and therefore the risk of detection may be as much, or a greater, deterrent than the penalty.

Some 'couriers' are of course accomplished performers but many others – particularly from the developing world – do aptly fit the descriptive but unflattering label of 'mules'. They are burdened from first to last, poorly educated, with personal circumstances which would be envied by absolutely no-one. However, the principle of deterrent sentencing – when taken to its logical conclusion – means that the personal circumstances of the accused are displaced, wholly or substantially, by the objective of using the defendant as a warning to others.[34] In *DPP v. Doot*, Lord Salmon said that great care is taken by most countries 'to do nothing which might help their own nationals to commit what would be crimes in other countries'. It is therefore no mitigation for a courier to say that the drug was intended for onward transmission to another country (and see *King*, November 23 1987, *The Times*).

The rationale of sentencing was perhaps most graphically explained by the former Lord Chief Justice, Lord Lane in *Aramah* (1982) 4 Cr.App.R.(S) 407 when he said of Class A drugs that:

Many of such criminals may think, and indeed do think, that it is less dangerous and more profitable to traffic in heroin or morphine than it is to rob a bank. It does not require much imagination to realise the consequential evils of corruption and bribery which the huge profits are likely to produce. [Thirdly], this factor is also important when considering the advisability of granting bail. Sums which to the ordinary person, and indeed the ordinary defendant, might seem enormous are often trivial for the trafficker in drugs. . . . [Fifthly, and lastly], and we have purposely left it for the last, because it is the most horrifying aspect, comes the degradation and suffering and not infrequently the death which the drug brings to the addict. It is not difficult to understand why in some part of the world traffickers in heroin in any substantial quantity are sentenced to death and executed.

Consequently anything which the courts of this country can do by way of deterrent sentences on those found guilty of crimes involving these Class 'A' drugs should be done. . . .

This, however, is one area in which it is particularly important that offenders should be encouraged to give information to the police, and a confession of guilt, coupled with considerable assistance to the police, can properly be marked by a substantial reduction in what would otherwise be the proper sentence. . . .

... The reason for this is, it is well known that the large scale operator looks for couriers of good character and for people of a sort which is likely to exercise the sympathy of the court if they are detected and arrested. Consequently one will frequently find students and sick and elderly people are used as couriers for two reasons: first of all they are vulnerable to suggestion and vulnerable to the offer of quick profit, and secondly, it is felt that the courts may be moved to misplaced sympathy in their case. There are few, if any, occasions when anything other than an immediate custodial sentence is proper in this type of importation.

The Court of Appeal has reiterated the sentencing policy of the courts to be one of deterrence and that credit will be given for pleas of guilty and assistance given to the law enforcement agencies: see *Aranguren and others* (1994) 99 Cr. App. R. 347 and *Warren and Beeley, The Times,* July 4, 1995.

Good Character

Both in *Aramah* (1982) 4 Cr.App.R.(S) 497, and in *Martinez* (1984) 6 Cr.App.R.(S) 364, it was said that the good character of the offender is seldom of any weight. This also applies to the personal circumstances of the defendant. The court remarked that such persons are usually selected to act as couriers because they are of good character. It is unlikely that the Court was seeking to justify or to explain the harshness of this result on those grounds – indeed, how could it logically do so: the vulnerability and the good character of the courier could only serve as mitigation in his or her case and yet it will often reflect in the culpability of the organiser if s/he should come to be sentenced.

Unfortunately, the harshness of the result is a consequence of the deterrent principle of sentencing. The fact that the drug is carried in a suitcase, ingeniously concealed in tins labelled 'fruit juice' or concealed in a converted petrol tank of a hired motor car may usefully serve to draw a sharp distinction between the courier and the organiser and such facts may offer some clues as to the reasons why the courier became involved in the venture.

Mitigating Factors

As a general rule, there are three main mitigating factors which can be expected to have a discernible impact on the sentence imposed: i) a plea of guilty; ii) assistance given to the officers; and iii) remorse coupled with the first two points. Other mitigating factors may include entrapment, and a defendant's genuine belief that the drug in question was of a type that attracts a lesser penalty than was in fact imported or transported.

i. Pleas of guilty

The well publicised policy of the courts is to give 'credit' (discount) for a plea of guilty.[35] A guilty plea may be evidence of a person's remorse for the commission of an offence but it does not always follow that a contested trial will inevitably result in a longer sentence being imposed.[36] However, in most cases, a discount for a plea of guilty is discernible and will be most apparent in cases where there are co-defendants some of whom plead guilty and others who are convicted after a trial. Assuming equal involvement between defendants, the benchmark will often be set by the convicted accused. Those who pleaded guilty will expect to see a significant reduction in their sentences – perhaps by as much as a third. Some courts give little credit where the evidence against the courier is regarded by the sentencer as overwhelming. A plea of guilty coupled with assistance given by an offender (particularly where that person has given evidence against confederates) may result in a substantial reduction in the sentence – perhaps by as much as a half.

ii. Assistance given to the authorities

Although sentencers will often be assisted by material contained in a Pre-Sentence Report,[37] many cases (resulting in a substantially lower sentence than might have been anticipated under the sentencing guidelines) are likely to be explained by mitigating factors other than personal circumstances. The best example is when the offender assists the law enforcement agencies. In order to protect the defendant in such circumstances, there is a well established and approved procedure for informing the court about the assistance which involves little being said directly in open court.[38] As a result, neither official statistics nor research studies can effectively reveal the proportion of cases where the sentence is discounted on that basis alone.

If a conviction prompts a defendant to give assistance to the law enforcement agencies, a delay between conviction and sentence may give the officers time to act on any information relayed by the offender. If the information proves to be valuable, that fact can be put before the court in mitigation. Irrespective as to whether the motive for cooperating is based on i) a genuine desire to help, or ii) remorse, or iii) represents a purely selfish interest on the part of the defendant to mitigate the sentence, the discount is likely to be the same – but the assistance given must be real. The earlier the defendant cooperates with the law enforcement officers, the more likely it is that the validity of the information can be demonstrated. Accordingly, the defendant's assistance will be more readily acknowledged by the court and is likely to be reflected in the sentence.

The courier who, as part of the criminal enterprise, agreed to meet the intended recipient of the drugs in this country, may decide to cooperate with officers and go ahead with that meeting under controlled conditions. It may lead to other arrests. Occasionally, the courier may decide to go further and to give evidence against co-defendants. The courts will reflect, in the sentence, the risks that ran with that decision. It follows that in cases where assistance has been given, and a plea of guilty entered, the discount on sentence may be substantial. In such a case a PSR may be of considerable assistance to the defendant if the overall picture presented to the judge is that of a courier who has expressed considerable remorse.

However, the extent to which credit is given for assistance is a matter for the sentencer: there is no set scale but the Court of Appeal may reduce a sentence where insufficient credit has been given: *Martin* (1994) 15 Cr.App.R.(S) 613. In other cases, it is sometimes difficult to tell whether any significant discount was given by the court but the usual inference is that the assistance was of little or of limited value: see *Hurst* (1989) 11 Cr.App.R.(S) 365.

iii. Mistaken belief as to the drug handled

Even though the maximum penalties for Class A, B and C drugs are different,[39] no distinction is made between different drugs in the same class for the purpose of sentencing. Thus, in *Suermondt* (1982) 4 Cr.App.R.(S) 5, it was said that even if cocaine is less dangerous and less socially harmful than heroin, there was little merit in distinguishing between the two types of drug.[40] In *Martinez* (1984) 6 Cr.App.R.(S) 346, the Court of Appeal remarked that 'any idea that those who import cocaine or LSD, as it is known, should be treated more leniently is wrong ... Anything which these courts can do to prevent [an upward spiral] will be done'. In *Warren & Beeley, The Times*, July 4 1995, the Court of Appeal held that the sentencing tariff for offences for ecstasy would be maintained at substantially the same level as in relation to other Class A controlled drugs. Similar considerations apply to LSD: *Kemp* (1979) 69 Cr.App.R. 330.

However, a courier's belief that a drug of a lesser Class was imported – or involves a different prohibited article altogether – may afford some mitigation: *Bilinski* (1988) 9 Cr.App.R.(S) 360; and see *Ashley* (1993) 14 Cr.App.R.(S) 581 and the court may conduct a hearing to determine that issue.[41] Similar considerations apply where the courier mistakenly believes that the drug is of low purity: *Varshney* (1985) 16 Cr.App.R.(S) 267.

A more difficult issue is whether a courier's mistaken belief can also serve to aggravate the sentence. In *Afzal & Arshad* (1992) 13 Cr.App.R.(S) 145, the appellants were found in possession of 1,236 grams of powder which they believed to be heroin. In fact the powder consisted of 1 percent diamorphine and was so dilute as to be unsaleable. The sentences of 12 years and 8 years were reduced to 8 years and 5 years respectively. The court rejected the proposition that the appellants should be sentenced on the basis that the substance was virtually valueless and remarked that the person who believed that the drug imported was of a greater purity than was in fact the case is more culpable than the person who believes that virtually unsaleable heroin has been imported.

Effect of Pre-Sentence Reports on sentence

The Criminal Justice Act 1991 imposed an obligation on courts to obtain Pre-Sentence Reports[42] in cases other than those which can only be tried on indictment. It may be that Parliament had not fully thought through the implications of that provision believing that all serious offences would come under the category of 'indictable only' offences. In fact, most drug-trafficking offences do not, procedurally, come under that heading and thus the courts were obliged to have a PSR in almost every case where an importer appeared to be sentenced. This has now changed with the passing of the Criminal Justice and Public Order Act 1994 but early indications suggest that the courts are asking for the preparation of a PSR in the majority of importation cases. This may be viewed with surprise if it is correct to say that social background information seldom carries any weight. Nicholas Hammond's comprehensive study on the value of Pre-Sentence Reports (see Hammond, this volume),[43] discovered just how important judges in the United Kingdom do regard deterrence in the sentencing of drug couriers. He cites a number of instances where judges have made it quite clear that the personal circumstances of the offending courier have little or no impact on the sentence passed. As one judge remarked 'It's largely a matter of mathematics really'. This must not be taken literally but it does reinforce the view that the offender's personal circumstances have little impact on the sentence passed in the majority of cases. That particular judge went on to say that the '. . . Appeal Court guidelines are guidelines, not tramlines, but unless there's any good reason to depart from them, I don't'.

The severity of this approach is illustrated in *Stark* [1992] Crim.L.R. 384 in which the court declined to reduce a sentence for an offence of possessing a controlled drug with intent to supply on the grounds that the offender had developed AIDS and had a very limited life expectancy.[44] So what is the point in having PSRs? The exercise is not necessarily academic. In *Veeraswamy* (1993) 14 Cr.App.R.(S) 680, a sentence of 5 years' imprisonment on a 36 year old woman convicted of possessing 50 Ecstasy tablets was reduced to 3 years on the grounds of personal hardship, namely the detrimental effect her imprisonment was having on her children. It had been held in *Parkinson* (unreported, November 4, 1976) that a court might mitigate a sentence to avoid exceptional hardship. However, that case was decided long before *Aramah* and on any view, *Veeraswamy* has to be viewed as the exception which proves the rule.

Foreign nationals: double jeopardy and deportation

There have been suggestions from commentators that foreign nationals, or persons with no community ties in the United Kingdom, are more likely to attract longer custodial sentences than British citizens charged with the same offence.[45] However, current research tends to suggest that sentencing is not influenced by the offender's nationality or status and that, despite the sentencing guidelines laid down by the Court of Appeal in respect of drug-trafficking offences, a greater flexibility of sentencing is demonstrated by the courts in dealing with drug couriers than might have been expected.[46]

Nevertheless, it is no mitigation in English law that a trafficker is liable to be sentenced abroad for an offence committed in this country. In *Nwoko* (1995) 16 Cr.App.R.(S) 612, a Nigerian national was sentenced to 5 years' imprisonment for her part in the unlawful importation of some 222 grams of cocaine. Under Nigerian decree 33, any Nigerian citizen convicted abroad of an offence involving narcotic drugs and who 'thereby brings the same Nigeria into disrepute is guilty of an offence and liable to a term of 5 years' imprisonment without an option of a fine' (see Joshua; and Stanley, this volume). The Court of Appeal rejected the submission that this placed her in double jeopardy for which some allowance should be made. What is unclear is the extent to which this decree is applied in practice. This issue must have been in the contemplation of the court when it remarked that the sentencing judge would be faced with an 'impossible task' in seeking to discover whether the decree would be applied in the defendant's case. In that case, the defendant had also been recommended for deportation and the existence of the Nigerian decree appears to have been considered by the court to be one matter which the Home Office could take into account when considering the question of deportation.

It is not unusual to find that couriers, who are not British citizens, (or who do not come within one of the statutory exceptions) are recommended for deportation even if they have not offended before.[47] It must be emphasized that although the sentencing court has no power to order deportation, a recommendation of the court is not going to be treated lightly by the Executive. The court's power to *recommend* deportation arises under section 6 of the Immigration Act 1971 whereas liability for deportation, in respect of a person who has committed a drug trafficking offence, may arise under two different statutory provisions.

The first is where the Secretary of State deems the person's deportation to be 'conducive to the public good'.[48] Under this head, the question of deportation may be considered even where the court makes no recommendation for deportation: *Butt v. Secretary of State* [1979] Imm.A.R. 82. The phrase 'conducive to the public good' is not defined by statute. Although regard may be had to compassionate circumstances, serious criminal offences (such as the supply or importation of a controlled drug) may result in deportation under this heading even if the defendant was of previous good character and unlikely to re-offend: see *R. v. Immigration Appeal Tribunal ex. p. Florent* [1985] Imm.A.R. 141.

The second, and typical case, is where the courier is recommended for deportation under sections 3(6) and 6 of the Immigration Act 1971. Neither section specifies the circumstances in which a court would be entitled to make such a recommendation. However, in *Nazari* 71 Cr.App.R. 87, the Court of Appeal firmly stated that the effect of a recommendation for deportation is 'to indicate to the Secretary of State that in the opinion of the court it is to the detriment of this country that the accused should remain here'. This is, perhaps, another way of saying that deportation would be 'conducive to the public good'. The fact of a conviction will not necessarily justify the court making a recommendation for deportation. The court is entitled to take into account the personal circumstances of the offender: *David* 2 Cr.App.R.(S) 362; and *Tshuma* (1981) 3 Cr.App.R.(S) 97.

Anecdotal accounts suggest that many recommendations for deportation, in respect of drug couriers, are made almost (if not totally) without comment or objection. The likely reason is that recommendations are perceived to be largely academic. 'Leave to enter' will probably be refused or revoked by the immigration authorities at the time the offender is apprehended, leading to the defendant being 'removed'[49] or 'deported' whether a recommendation for deportation is made or not. Moreover, the making of a recommendation for deportation will not reduce the sentence imposed for the offence (see Stanley, this volume).[50]

Conclusion

Unhappily, little research has been undertaken on the sentencing of drug couriers. However, we need to understand the implications of present sentencing practice and the policy which informs it. Tracy Huling suggests that we should 'face squarely the likelihood that our drug-war strategies, adjusted by many other notions, have so far resulted only in the re-victimisation of many people already suffering under grinding poverty and corrupt political regimes'. Few, surely, could argue with that proposition in so far as it concerns the drug 'mule'. Likewise, few could disagree that prison serves the courier no personal benefit or dispute the severe hardship that prison sentences cause to innocent third parties including family and friends who, perversely perhaps, the courier intended to help. Some courts do temper their sentences to take into account such hardship (see *Veeraswamy*, 14 Cr.App.R.(S) 680) but others feel unable to do so on the grounds that it would be inconsistent with the principle of deterrent sentencing set out in *Aramah* and other cases.

Legalization and decriminalization are options but they are not on the legislative agenda in the UK nor, frankly, are they likely to be – no matter which political party is in power. The present Government is firmly set against legalization.[51] Even if a government was sympathetic to legalization or decriminalization of some, or all, controlled drugs the reality is that no one country is going to unilaterally act in a way that will be construed as reneging on a Convention or a Treaty to which it was a party – particularly if that country was an active participant in the debates and would thus risk (a) undermining it's own credibility internationally by failing to honour its international agreements and (b) would consider itself as removing the lid from the top of a pot, uncertain as to what the results would be and fearing that it may be too late to put the lid back on again if the contents over-reacted.

In the Government White Paper, *Tackling Drugs Together*, it is said that if the United Kingdom decided to break its international obligations there is a danger that it could become a major centre for drug trafficking, money laundering and associated crime. These claims must be examined seriously. It is also said that the 'strongest arguments against legalization of controlled drugs are the risks of wider use and addiction'. This is much more contentious: can drug use really get much wider? As a way of seeking to introduce some measure of compromise, some countries have sought to alter their domestic laws without breaking their international obligations. In Britain, cautioning offenders requires an admission of guilt, but it is an administrative process that avoids an appearance at court. It is a form of de-criminalization in the sense only that a caution is not recorded as a conviction and therefore attracts no penalty.

In the Netherlands, the authorities have gone very much further but, as we have seen, its actions have not been met with approval from other countries who see any problem removed from the Dutch interior as being merely transferred elsewhere. However, it is reported that there is little drug related crime in the Netherlands and that a relaxation of drug enforcement has not resulted in soaring addiction so that addiction is lower there than in either Italy or the United Kingdom.[52] Nevertheless, the Netherlands is a major centre for drug trafficking and a staging-post for the onward transmission of drugs. Many Dutch nationals act as couriers for the transportation of Class A and Class B drugs to this country. In the absence of precise data it would be imprudent to speculate as to the proportion of couriers who could be appropriately described as 'mules'. Nevertheless, the majority are persons who have no criminal record. What is clear beyond a shadow of doubt is that the number of drug seizures has increased significantly over the years.

In the last ten years, steps have also been taken in the UK to tackle drug-money-laundering through the recovery of illgotten gains and taking funds out of circulation which could be used to finance further criminal ventures. This is an international effort. It is an attempt to tackle international crime by attacking the profit element and it is also an attempt to strike at the organisers by making it more difficult for them to remain undetected (if drug funds can be traced to them) or at least to remove their funds from

110

their control. If it is effective, then, in theory, the chain of supply collapses and the use of couriers thus becomes redundant. This, at least, is the theory.

Notes

1. *Regina v Taylor and Dhorat*: Dhorat was convicted after a trial and he was also sentenced to 18 months' imprisonment.
2. *Hussain* (1969) 53 Cr. App. R. 448.
3. *Bilinski* (1988) 9 Cr. App. R.(S) 360 and see *Ashley* (1993) 14 Cr. App. R.(S) 581; and *Varshney* (1995) 16 Cr. App. R.(S) 267.
4. Saturday, September 9th, 1995.
5. Monday, September 25th, 1995.
6. *Drugs, Crime and Corruption* 1995, MacMillan Press.
7. Drugswatch: *Just Say No*; Corgi Books, 1986.
8. Cm 2678; p. 92; table A. vii.
9. and see *Drugs, Crime and Corruption*, Richard Clutterbuck, 1995.
10. The capsule form of the drug was banned by the Department of Health on 18 October 1995.
11. *Drugs, Crime and Corruption*, MacMillan, 1995.
12. *The Economist*, 1994, p. 22.
13. *The Economist*, November 13, 1993, p. 38.
14. See *Hussain* (1969) 53 Cr. App. R. 448 in respect of importation offences and *McNamara* (1988) 152 JP 390 in respect of offences under the Misuse of Drugs Act 1971.
15. Penny Green, *Drug Couriers*, Howard League for Penal Reform, 1991.
16. Report of a Study Tour of Nigeria, 1992 MAPS.
17. The Characteristics and Sentencing of Illegal Drug Importers, Brit. J. Criminal. Vol 34 No. 4, 1994.
18. *Drugs, Crime and Corruption*, 1995, p. 66 and p. 161.
19. See *Crack of Doom*, Jon Silverman, Headline, 1994.
20. *Drugs, Crime and Corruption*, 1995, p. 144.
21. (1982) 4 Cr. App. R.(S) 407.
22. And see the commentary to *Patel* [1987] Crim. L. R. 838.
23. *Hansard* H.I. Vol 527, col. 1563, Vol 527, col. 93; H.C. Vol. 193 col. 866.
24. See the *Report of the Proceedings of the Judicial Conference of the United States*, March 13, 1990.
25. *Women Drug Couriers*; Criminal Justice; ABA, winter 1995, col. 9, No. 4, Section of Criminal Justice.
26. *An Analysis of Non-Violent Drug Offenders with Minimal Criminal Histories* (1994).
27. Huling, *Women Drug Couriers* (1995).
28. Cannabis and cannabis resin are separately listed in Part II to Sch. 2 of the Misuse of Drugs Act 1971. 'Cannabis' is of herbal variety.
29. 105 State Papers 490.
30. Cmd. 3244.
31. Cmd. 4413 ie. the *Convention for Limiting the Manufacture and Regulating the Distribution of Narcotic Drugs*.

32. Defined as the 'dried flowering and fruiting tops of the . . . cannabis sativa'.
33. Dangerous Drugs Act (Application) Order 1946 S.R. & O. 1946 No. 2018.
34. And see *Rospigliosi* [1980] Crim.L.R. 664.
35. See *Aramah* (1982) 4 Crim. App. R.(S) 407.
36. See footnote 1.
37. See *Drug Couriers: a Role for the Probation Service* (1992). *The Value of Pre-Sentence Reports on Foreign Nationals* (1994) M.P.S.
38. See *Sivan & Others* and see *Kliteze* (1995) 16 Cr.App.R.(S) 445.
39. Class A – life, Class B – 14 years; Class C = 5 years. Misuse of Drugs Act 1971 (as amended).
40. And see *Ford* (1981) 3 Cr.App.R.(S) 70.
41. *Newton* (1988) 4 Cr.App.R.(S) 388.
42. ie. for the purposes of obtaining social background information.
43. *The Value of Pre-Sentence Reports on Foreign Nationals* (1994) MPS.
44. And see *Moore* (1990) 12 Cr.App.R.(S) 384; and see also *Roby*; transcript April 29, 1993, C.A.
45. *A Study of Foreign Prisoners*; I.L.P.S.
46. Green, P., Mills, C. and Read, T., *British Journal of Criminology*; Vol. 35, No. 4, 1994.
47. The defendant must be at least 17 years of age and convicted of an offence punishable with imprisonment: see s. 3(6) and s. 6 of the Immigration Act 1971.
48. Section 3(5)(b) Immigration Act 1971.
49. See para. 9 of Sch. 2, Immigration Act 1971 and see *R. v. Immigration Officer, ex. p. Shah* [1982] 2 All E.R. 264.
50. *Edgehill*, 47 Cr.App.R. 41.
51. See the White Paper *Talking Drugs Together* (1994) C, 2678.
52. Annex D.7.

2
Deportation and Drugs Couriers

Alison Stanley

Introduction

The position of the two young women, recently released from a Thai prison after serving 2 years for attempting to smuggle out large quantities of heroin, met with an ambivalent reaction from the media in the UK. No such ambivalence is shown to foreign nationals convicted of drugs in the UK. On the contrary, the harsh sentences meted out by virtue of the automatic tariff (where the sentence is linked to the alleged street value or weight of the drugs) and the routine deportation from the UK on the completion of sentence meets with almost universal approval. The reason for this consensus is based in the so called 'war on drugs' conducted by Northern nations. Certainly, the international drugs trade is a major concern for governments.

The number of foreign nationals

Significant numbers of foreign nationals are involved in drugs couriering. The number of foreign nationals convicted and imprisoned in the UK (about 1250) and the percentage (about 39%) of foreign nationals imprisoned for drugs offences has remained more or less constant over the past few years.[1] Of the foreign nationals being held in prison department establishments on 28 February 1993, 680 people were recorded as being under sentence for drugs offences, that is 27 percent of the total population under sentence for drugs offences.[2] These figures include all types of drugs offences. Although there are no official statistics, two recent studies have shown that the majority of those 341, convicted of the illegal importation of controlled drugs, are foreign nationals. Penny Green's 1991 study points to 72 percent of her sample of those imprisoned for the illegal importation of drugs being foreign nationals[3] and this is reinforced by the study carried out by Middlesex Area Probation Service which found 65 percent of their sample of cases committed to Isleworth Crown Court were foreign nationals.[4]

Sentencing: double punishment

Many foreign nationals claim that they are more harshly sentenced than their British equivalents.[5] This notion has not been confirmed by research but what is uncontestable is the fact that foreign nationals face a double punishment of expulsion from the UK at the end of their sentence.

A foreign national aged over 17 convicted of drugs couriering will not only be sentenced to the steep tariff penalty of imprisonment as set down in the case of *Aramah*[6] and revised in the leading case of *Bilinski*[7] but will, almost invariably, also be thrown out of the UK. It is the usual practice of the courts to impose this further punishment on foreign nationals. Under section 3(6) of the Immigration Act 1971 a foreign national is liable for deportation if he or she is not a British citizen, a Commonwealth citizen with the right of abode, or a Commonwealth citizen with the right of abode, or a Commonwealth citizen settled in the UK on 1.1.1973[8] and who has lived in the UK for a minimum of 5 years since that date. Such a person can be recommended for deportation if convicted of an imprisonable criminal offence. This applies to foreign nationals regardless of their immigration status, although people recognised as refugees under the 1951 United Nations Convention relating to the status of refugees (but not those granted 'exceptional leave to remain') are in effect not deportable, nor are recognised diplomats who are exempt from immigration control under the Diplomatic Privileges Act 1964. This means that, as the Double Punishment campaign states, a person could be resident in the UK for '15 weeks or 15 years' but still be recommended for deportation by the sentencing court.

Workers and self-employed people from European Community countries are subject to limited immigration control and can only be deported on grounds of 'public policy, public health and public security'.[9] However, the international consensus surrounding the importers of controlled drugs places them squarely in the 'public policy' exception and thus EC nationals can, and are, deported for all types of drugs offences, other than simple possession.

Deportation guidelines

As the recommendation for deportation forms part of the sentence, the only right of appeal is through the normal criminal justice system of appeal against conviction and/or sentence.[10] Case law has made it clear that deportation should not follow routinely when a foreign national, liable for deportation is convicted.

The guidelines for whether a recommendation for deportation is appropriate are contained in the leading case of *Nazari*,[11] in which one of the appellants was an Iranian convicted of the illegal importation of controlled drugs. This case makes it clear that a recommendation for deportation should not be made automatically, or as an 'afterthought'. Instead, the court should consider two factors; firstly whether the person's continued presence in the UK is a detriment to the UK; and secondly the effect of a recommendation on innocent third parties, such as family members. In addition, the court stated that when considering a recommendation for deportation, the courts will not be concerned with the political system in the offender's home country; such factors being a matter for the Home Secretary alone. This last factor has particular relevance for asylum seekers as it means that the full motives behind drugs importing are not always examined by the courts.

Thus the court should weigh up the gravity of the offence against the individual's record and circumstances. In drugs couriering cases, the courts consistently regard the offence as so serious that deportation is always the appropriate course, even if it is a first offence.

However, it is not the courts who make the final decision:

the court's recommendation is only that, a recommendation. The decisive determination rests with the Secretary of State for the Home Department. However, the statistics show that the Home Office rarely ignores a court's recommendation for deportation. In 1992 the Home Office decided *not* to implement the court's recommendation in only 29 cases while 284 deportation orders were made pursuant to a court's recommendation.[12]

Before reaching a conclusion about what is to be a very grave step (and the significance of deportation is demonstrated by the legislators of the Immigration Rules ensuring that the Order for deportation itself must be signed by a Secretary of State personally[13]), the Home Office is obliged to consider the 'public interest' in deporting someone 'balanced against any compassionate circumstances of the case' and there must be consistency in the exercise of these rules.[14] The Secretary of State must take into account all the relevant factors which are set out in paragraph 364 of the Immigration Rules.[15] These include the prospective deportee's age; length of residence in the UK; strength of connections with the UK; personal history, including character, conduct and employment record; domestic circumstances; the nature of the offence for which the person was convicted; previous criminal record; compassionate circumstances; and any representations received on the person's behalf. However, the most important factor in the case of drugs couriers is the nature of the offence, which invariably outweighs the other compassionate factors.

If the Home Office decides to implement the court's recommendation, then there is no further right of appeal within the immigration appeals system (apart from a technical right of appeal against the destination to which it is proposed to deport the individual).[16] Following the *Nazari* guidelines the courts normally impose a recommendation for deportation, but even if they fail to do so the Home Office can still initiate deportation action against a foreign national convicted of drugs couriering on the basis that his or her continued presence in the UK is not conducive to the public good.[17] However, contrary to the position of a person recommended for deportation by a court, the foreign national does have a right of appeal within the immigration appeal system. Uniquely, the appeal is heard, not by an Adjudicator, the first strata of the appeal system, but by an Immigration Appeal Tribunal, thus precluding any further appeals, should the initial appeal be unsuccessful.

Once again, the factors contained in paragraph 364 of the Immigration Rules are rehearsed. However, in cases concerning the illegal importation of drugs, the apparently universal consensus over drugs couriers prevails and the Immigration Appeal Tribunal is reluctant to overturn the Home Office's decision. This is graphically illustrated by the situation of Andy Anderson, a Jamaican citizen and Rastafarian, who had lived in the UK for eleven years before he and his British citizen partner were convicted of cannabis possession with intent to supply. Although he was not convicted of importing the response of the Immigration Appeal Tribunal was unremitting. Despite the fact that his partner, twin sons, all his family (mother and sisters) live in the UK and that the sentencing judge had not recommended his deportation, the Home Office initiated deportation action on the basis that his presence in the UK was not conducive to the public good. This decision was upheld by the Tribunal who stated that despite it being 'obvious that a number of experienced and impartial people including a Prison Governor, Probation Officer, Prison Chaplain and Education Officer have formed views of the appellant and believe he has turned over a new leaf', nevertheless, the Tribunal concluded '... after having seen the appellant in the witness stand and looking at the evidence as a whole ... (he) is likely to continue to earn his living by supplying drugs to other persons ... (as this) plays a significant part in the appellant's scheme of things'. It is hard not to agree with the Andy and Farida Anti-deportation Campaign in their conclusion that the Tribunal was influenced by Andy's appearance (dreadlocks), his accent and a misconception of the tenets of Rastafarian belief.[18]

The official consensus

The harsh effect in human terms of the consensus over drugs couriers is epitomised by the case of a Colombian man married for 15 years to a Bolivian woman, with two British citizen children, who came to the UK on work permits in 1974, and became legally settled in 1978. He was convicted of supplying a controlled drug (cocaine) and sentenced to 5 years in custody. Although the court did not recommend that he should be deported, the Home Office made a decision to deport him under s.3(5)(b) of the Immigration Act on the basis that his presence in this country was not conducive to the public good. His appeal was dismissed, despite the strong recommendations made by his wider family, employers, probation officer and family priest, and he has now left the UK thus being forcibly separated from his wife and children.[19]

That the consensus extends beyond the UK is illustrated by recent developments in European Law. Article 8 of the European Convention on Human Rights protects the right to respect for family and private life. Recently there has been a number of cases taken under Article 8 in which the European Court has held that the deportation of long term, legally resident foreign nationals with families in their country of residence, and no continuing connection with their country of origin, interferes with the individual's rights to family life.[20] This held for those who had committed criminal offences, even a series of offences. It is clear, however, that offences involving drugs fall outside this concession. This is reinforced by the recently leaked Home Office document containing secret instructions to Home Office officials on enforcement of immigration control by deportation in which the Home Office states that when 'removal can be justified as necessary in the interests of a democratic society' it can still take place. This would usually be after conviction for serious crimes and amongst the Home Office's illustrative list of such crimes appears 'drug offences (other than possession)'.[21]

The role of immigration control

The legal position is complicated by the fact that the majority of drugs couriers are detected by Customs and Excise at the port of entry, or shortly thereafter, and thus *after* they have gone through immigration control. An individual's leave to enter the UK can be revoked up to 24 hours after grant[22] and this usually occurs to foreign national drugs couriers detected shortly after entry. Thus the individual (although being held in a UK prison) has not technically been granted leave to enter. At the end of the sentence the individual can be ejected from the UK on two grounds: firstly as she or he has never been granted leave to enter and secondly, pursuant to a deportation order. This creates a legal conundrum for a person can only be *deported* from the UK if he or she has, at some stage, been legally present in the UK. Thus the legality of a deportation order made in such circumstances is unclear. However, the reasons for the government wishing to deport a foreign national in such circumstances, rather than merely eject him or her as a person who has been refused leave to enter, is clear. A deportation order, once signed, lasts indefinitely and the individual is effectively excluded from the UK for ever. In addition, in cases where no conviction is secured, the person can still be removed as he or she has been refused leave to enter.

It is possible to apply for a deportation order to be revoked, but the Home Office will not normally do this unless the person has been out of the UK for a minimum of 3 years and, in the case of people with a serious criminal record, until the person has been out of the UK for 'a long term of years'.[23] This is usually taken by the Home Office to be when the offence has been 'spent' within the meaning of the Rehabilitation of Offenders Act 1974. The types of sentence drugs couriers attract (Green found the average sentence for illegal importation of drugs was 6 years and 4 months) can never be 'spent' and this means offenders are effectively excluded indefinitely unless there are very strong compassionate circumstances. The case of an Iranian student illustrates this: Mr Z was recommended for deportation following his conviction for illegal drug importation, and despite his subsequent marriage to a British woman he was deported. His wife followed him to Iran where life for a British citizen became increasingly difficult, as anti-British sentiment rose, particularly after the delivery of the fatwa against Salman Rushdie. Mrs Z suffered health problems and wanted to return to the UK for fertility treatment not available in Iran. Mr Z had no further involvement in drugs, completed compulsory military service and started a business. Eventually, ten years after the deportation order was made, it was revoked and Mr Z successfully applied to return to the UK. The couple are now living in the UK with their daughter and running a thriving business.

Repatriation

The Repatriation of Prisoners Act 1984 enables the ratification of international treaties on prisoner transfer to enable long-term prisoners to carry out their sentence in their own country. However, reciprocal arrangements currently do not operate between the UK and the countries whose nationals form the majority of foreign offenders convicted of illegal importation of controlled drugs. According to both Green (1991) and Abernethy and Hammond (1992) the majority of foreign convicted drugs importers are from Nigeria, other parts of Africa and Colombia. No repatriation arrangement exists with any of these countries.

Home leave and parole[24]

A prospective deportee is able to apply for home leave and parole in the same way as any other prisoner. The head of the Home Office's Parole Unit has stated that the Local Review Committee or the Parole Board, when considering an application for parole, assumes that the home circumstances of a prospective deportee are satisfactory.[25] However Tarzi and Hedges concluded that within the Probation Service there was 'a consensus that the present parole system does discriminate against foreign offenders because of its reliance on Home Circumstance Assessment and supervised licence'[26] and it is clear that the chances of being granted parole are affected by the fact that the individual faces deportation. The rationale appears to be a consideration of the likelihood of the individual conforming to the terms of his or her release.

The view that prospective deportees are more likely to abscond is mirrored in the current policy of not considering prospective deportees for category D (open) prisons. This is clearly discriminatory, as not only is the general regime in category D prisons more relaxed, but there are also more opportunities for pre-release assistance and leave. This type of leave is aimed at assisting prisoners in re-adapting to outside life, and this is as relevant to those who are to be deported as to any other prisoner. Generally, home leave (which is technically available to all prisoners), is commonly denied to prospective deportees. Deborah Cheney quotes one prisoner in this position, serving an 8 year sentence:

> If I was an English prisoner, I would have been going on home leave for quite some time now ... yet the reality is that after four and a half years in prison without any family visits whatsoever ... I am still imprisoned, isolated in a different culture than the one I am accustomed to.[27]

Currently, many drugs offenders are serving sentences of more than five years and as such are affected by the 1983 decision of the Home Secretary that those serving more than five years for offences of sex, drugs or violence would only be eligible for a short period of parole (in practice 8 months), unless there were exceptional circumstances.

The Criminal Justice Act 1991 altered the framework for parole by abolishing remission and ensuring that all prisoners will spend at least half their sentence in prison. For short sentence prisoners (ie up to 4 years) release will then be automatic. For long sentence prisoners (ie over 4 years) a discretionary system of parole will remain. However, prospective deportees will be dealt with differently from other prisoners. Prospective deportees have the same rights to apply for 'early release' as other prisoners, but under s.46 of the Act, applications for parole by long sentence prisoners are not considered by the Parole Board but by the Home Secretary. In addition, they are not subject to post-release supervision by a probation officer. Instead, the individual will be deported once paroled. Although the new scheme only came into effect recently, the Home Office has started to use its powers to order early release and deportation. By 13 November 1993, 93 convicted deportees were granted early release.[28]

The administration of deportation orders

Drugs offenders, in common with other post conviction deportees, frequently serve additional time in custody as the machinery for deporting individuals is not always initiated at a sufficiently early stage. Thus once a prospective deportee's sentence is completed, unless he or she is released on parole, he or she will normally be detained under Immigration Act powers and transferred to the remand wing of a prison, or to HMP Haslar, the 'immigration prison'.[29]

The delay in administration of deportation orders mirrors the delay in arranging for transfer of prisoners under the Repatriation of Prisoners' Act, although in this instance the blame can usually be placed with the Home Office. It can cause immense distress to the deportee and his or her family. A current example concerns a Jamaican woman convicted of couriering drugs and recommended for deportation as part of her sentence. About two years before the end of her sentence she was served with a deportation order and directions for her removal to Jamaica. The deportation order, however, was technically incorrect and when her lawyers challenged its validity the Home Office eventually conceded this and withdrew it, stating it would be re-issued and re-served in the near future.

Despite the delay on the Home Office's part, her solicitors were given a typically short period (14 days) in which to submit representations on compassionate grounds of her circumstances. As a result of Home Office delay, she spent further time in custody at the end of her sentence before the Home Office sorted out the administrative muddle. In the meantime, her son in Jamaica, who had not seen his mother for several years, was separated from her for several months more. It is unacceptable that people should be imprisoned for longer than their sentence and is yet a further example of the discriminatory treatment suffered by foreign prisoners.

The costs of deportation will be met by the Home Office, but a prisoner's own cash can be used to defray the costs. This is often not explained to deportees who feel that they are being punished yet again for their offence, over and above their sentence of imprisonment.

Asylum seekers as couriers

A small but significant minority of people convicted of illegal importation of drugs do so as a means of acquiring sufficient money to enable them to flee from a country where they fear persecution. In these circumstances, drugs are being used as a form of hard currency by desperate individuals. Under the 1951 United Nations Convention relating to the status of refugees, a person can be excluded from applying for asylum if he or she has committed a 'serious non-political crime outside the country of refuge prior to his admission to that country as a refugee'.[30]

Clearly, by attempting to smuggle illegal drugs, prospective refugees have committed a crime both under UK law and outside the UK. This does not preclude them from applying for asylum at any stage but if they attempt to put forward facts relating to an asylum claim in mitigation in an attempt to avoid a recommendation for deportation after conviction, these will be ignored by the court under the *Nazari* guidelines outlined above.

If people are recommended for deportation, then they will only have an appeal against the destination to which it is proposed to remove them to (almost invariably this means the person's country of nationality, which in turn is the country from which the asylum seeker has fled). If asylum is refused, this appeal will be heard with the asylum appeal, under section 8 of the Asylum and Immigration Appeals Act 1993.

The Handbook on Procedure and Criteria for Determining Refugee Status accepts that 'serious crime' is difficult to define, but that it must be a capital crime or a very grave punishable act before an individual can be excluded from the protection of the Refugee Convention. The Handbook also acknowledges the position of people who commit a crime as a means of escape from the country where persecution is feared. A balance must be made, and the Home Office has allowed some people convicted of attempting to import illegal drugs as a means of escaping persecution to remain in the UK on an exceptional basis.

An instance is Mr BN, a young Tamil from Sri Lanka who was detected in transit at Gatwick Airport carrying a quantity of heroin. He was convicted of illegal importation and recommended for deportation at the end of his sentence. The court refused to take into account the reasons for his involvement in drug importing. Mr BN had been recruited by the Tamil Tigers at the age of 18, in 1982. He became actively involved in the civil war but by 1986 he was disillusioned with the policies and tactics of the Tigers and fled to India. There he felt increasingly under threat, as commitment to the Tigers is for life, and he feared reprisals for leaving the organization. Unable to raise the money to flee India, he agreed, in desperation, to carry drugs in exchange for a false passport and a ticket to Canada. A deportation order was made pursuant to the court's recommendation and Mr BN appealed against the directions for removal to Sri Lanka, where he feared his life would be in danger as a known member of the Tigers. He was released on bail by the immigration appellate authorities whilst his application for asylum was considered by the Home Office. This story ended happily, as he formed a close relationship with a British woman and the couple had a child together. Eventually, over two years after he had completed his sentence, the Home Office allowed Mr BN to remain in the UK on an exceptional basis.

Non-asylum seekers

Similar understanding has not been shown by the Home Office, however, for non-asylum seekers convicted of drugs offences from countries where such offences result in the death penalty. For example, Amnesty International believes that some people convicted of drugs offences in the UK who have been deported to Iran have been executed.[31] This has not prevented the Home Office from deporting others and it is significant that the leading case of *Nazari*, concerning court recommendations, related to a claim by the appellant that he would probably be executed on his return to Iran.

Similarly, the fact that Nigerian citizens convicted of drugs offences face the possibility of further imprisonment upon departation under Decree 33 is not taken into account either by the courts or the Home Office. In an attempt to discourage drug trafficking from its border, the Nigerian government has created two new offences by amending the National Drug Law Enforcement Agency (amended) Decree 1990 (known as Decree 33). The first offence is committed by any person whose journey originates from Nigeria and who is found to have imported drugs into another country, notwithstanding any court proceedings in the foreign country. Secondly, a Nigerian citizen found guilty abroad of a drugs offence, thus bringing Nigeria's name into disrepute, is also guilty of an offence. Both offences carry a sentence of five years and forfeiture of assets. Decree 33 was issued on 10th October

1990, and affects all Nigerian citizens who are convicted of drugs offences in the UK after that date. Decree 33 is not strictly double jeopardy, but it has the effects of punishing a person twice for the same act. As Nigerians form the largest national group of foreign convicted drugs couriers,[32] it is likely that Decree 33 will affect a significant number of people, although its precise effect is not yet clear, given the lengthy sentences imposed on couriers.

Discrimination against foreign nationals

The courts have made it clear that the United Kingdom 'has no use for criminals of other nationalities, particularly if they have committed serious crimes or have long criminal records'.[33] However, the claim that the 'final decision is for the Secretary of State' is somewhat hollow, given the Home Office's almost automatic implementation of court recommendations to deport.

Immigration control is designed to exclude black people from the UK and to control their movements once within the UK. The racist nature of immigration control is clear both in the development of statute and case law over the past thirty years and in the application of the law to black people. Although the majority of people convicted of drugs offences in the UK are British citizens (and make up a significant proportion of those convicted of drugs importing[34]), foreign offenders receive harsher treatment. Foreign nationals liable to deportation, who are convicted of illegal importation of controlled drugs, are invariably recommended for deportation as part of their sentence and this recommendation is usually followed.

As well as this additional sentence, and as a direct consequence of their status as 'prospective deportees', they suffer further punishment and discriminatory treatment through restricted access to home leave and parole. This cannot be justified in the interests of the government's 'war on drugs' and is a clear demonstration of the link between the criminal justice system and the system of immigration control. There are signs that the universal support for long sentences for drugs offenders is beginning to disintegrate. Even mainstream conservatives such as Sir John Wheeler have begun to accept that 'it is absurd to argue that imposing lengthy prison sentences on poverty-stricken Third World women will help stamp out the drugs trade'.[35] A more humane attitude to foreign drugs offenders is necessary and this must include a speedier administrative system of deportations and the removal of all discriminatory measures which act as additional punishments.

Notes

1. The number of foreign nationals convicted each year, and the percentage of which were for drugs offences is as follows:
   1990: 1248   39%
   1989: 1192   39%
   1988: 1097   38%
   1987: 1172   36%
   1986: 886   32%
   Hansard 3.6.91, col.84.
2. Hansard 19.11.91 col.107.
3. Dr Penny Green, 'Drug Couriers', 1990, Howard League for Penal Reform.
4. Rosemary Abernethy and Nick Hammond, 'Drug Couriers: a role for the probation service', 1992, Middlesex Area Probation Service, pp. 35–6.
5. See Aysha Tarzi and John Hedges, A prison within a prison, ILPS, 1990, p. 54.
6. 4 Cr App R (s) 407.
7. 86 Cr App R 146.
8. Immigration Act 1971 s.7.
9. Directive 63/360/EEC, Article 10.
10. Immigration Act 1971 s.5(5).
11. [1980] 3 All ER 880.
12. Home Office Statistical Bulletin, issue 14/93.
13. The requirement for personal signature by the Secretary of State of all deportation orders appeared in the previous Immigration Rules (HC 251 para. 175). However, the revised consolidated rules currently in force (HC 395) have no such requirement. Despite this, there has been no change in practice. Nevertheless, the removal of the requirement for personal signature by the Secretary of State appears to remove a high level safeguard. In practice, the amount of protection provided by this procedure is minimal.
14. Immigration Rules HC 251, para 162.
15. HC 251.
16. These appeals rarely succeed as third countries are reluctant to accept deportees, particularly following conviction.
17. Immigration Act 1971 s.3(5)(b).
18. See Andy and Farida Anti-deportation Campaign and Greater Manchester Immigration Aid Unit, A long sharp shock.
19. Unless otherwise noted, the cases referred to in this article are all from the writer's own casework when detention worker/solicitor at the Joint Council for the Welfare of Immigrants.
20. Moustaquim v Belgium 13 Part 6 1991 EHRR p.802, Beldoudi v France 55/1990/246/317, Djeroud v France 34/1990/225/289.
21. Sue Shutter and Nuala Mole, Briefing on Home Office Instructions on Deportation, Immigration Law Practitioners' Association, 16.6.1993.

22. Immigration Act 1971, schedule 2 s.6(2).
23. Immigration Rules HC 251 para 180.
24. This article was written before the extensive restrictions to temporary release introduced by the Prison Service Instruction to Governors, IG36/95, were implemented on 25 April 1995.
25. Norman McLean at a meeting of the Save the Children's West African offenders practice issues group, 25.3.1992.
26. Tarzi and Hedges, ibid. p. 56.
27. Deborah Cheney, Into the dark tunnel, Prison Reform Trust, 1993, p. 29.
28. Hansard 3.6.1991 col. 84.
29. Since this article was written, in addition to HMP Haslar, HMP Rochester has opened a dedicated wing for Immigration Act prisoners. Campsfield House, run by Group 4 Security, has also been opened solely for Immigration Act detainees. Other detention facilities are being planned.
30. Article 1 F(b).
31. Amnesty International, Iran: over 900 executions announced in 5 months, June 1989, AI index: MDE 13/19/89.
32. Green, ibid. p.5.
33. *Nazari* ibid.
34. British citizens make up 28.3% of Green's sample (Green, ibid p.9) and 34% of the Middlesex Area Probation Service's sample (Abernethy and Hammond, ibid. p. 35).
35. Quoted in *The Independent* 22.7.1993.

3
A Prison Within a Prison – 4 Years On: An Overview

John Hedge and Ayesha Tarzi

Introduction

All offenders, British or otherwise, encounter problems during their custodial period. The major difference for foreign offenders is that the problems are more acute, exacerbated by cultural difference and their lack of awareness of the system in which they find themselves.

There are approximately 3000 foreign offenders in custody in the United Kingdom. Of the 50 percent serving sentences for drug related offences, most are from South America, West Africa and South Asia.

As drug trafficking is clearly linked with poverty, falling commodity prices, debt and political instability, the number of couriers coming from specific countries in the above mentioned regions, tends to fluctuate in accordance with current economic and political events.

A comprehensive study of the needs and problems of foreign prisoners in British prisons was carried out by us in 1989–1990. The findings published by the Inner London Probation Service in the form of a report titled 'A Prison Within a Prison' were based on information gleaned from interviews with 234 male and female prisoners from 50 different countries.

Special hardships

Our report identified the range of particular difficulties and special hardships encountered by foreign prisoners in English prisons and suggested a number of policy options for the various Criminal Justice agencies dealing with foreign prisoners. There is no doubt from subsequent research that their problems remain the same. A considerable amount of work has subsequently been undertaken however and the purpose of this article is to assess the progress made and identify those areas which will need significant longer term attention.

Foreign prisoners face different problems depending on their religion, culture, gender and country of origin. The problems of Asian prisoners differ from those of European/Western prisoners, who in turn do not share some of the particular problems experienced by Africans or South Americans. European/Western prisoners are more likely to understand about UK legal procedures in view of the similarity of the system with their own. They are also more aware of the services they are entitled to and their general rights. Asian and African prisoners are discouraged as they have no knowledge of the system or their rights. European/Western prisoners are in most cases saved the worry about their families as there are well established support and welfare services in their own countries. For Asians and Africans, the anxiety about family welfare can be overwhelming.

One of the most distressing and intractable difficulties prisoners from certain cultural backgrounds have to contend with is that of the prison stigma. In the Latin, Asian and African cultures, the stigma of being in prison has grave and far reaching consequences, not only for the prisoner but for his or her family. Serving time abroad is seen as a disgrace with attendant loss of respect. All those directly related to the prisoner suffer as a result. The break up of marriages, engagements and other relationships, disruption of education, loss of employment, problems with the children and social ostracism are among the most serious consequences. In many instances the prisoner's family is ostracised by the society in which they live and in turn reject the prisoner. It does not matter whether, as frequently happens, the courier has committed the offence for the sole purpose of obtaining funds to support the family – he or she is still seen as being guilty of dishonouring the family name. Many prisoners appear to be far more distressed about the possibility of family rejection than the prospect of facing a long term of imprisonment. A sense of powerlessness, fed by isolation and the lack of accurate or up-to-date information from home frequently adds to the sense of guilt and shame.

One of the most notable findings of our research was the experience which many prisoners, regardless of cultural and religious differences, had of poor legal representation and a lack of information about the process of Criminal Justice, and its consequences for them. Language difficulties arose as a particular problem. There is little evidence to suggest much improvement in this area and it remains a major concern. Since a substantial proportion of the cases concerned centre on major airports and their local courts, a targeted approach to improving matters is possible but the will to change things is necessary, and at present the legal profession has been unwilling to see this concern as a priority.

As far as other issues are concerned, family related problems of a financial or emotional nature are predominant. Over half of the prisoners interviewed for 'A Prison Within a Prison' expressed major worries in relation to their families.

This was particularly the case with African and Asian prisoners, most of whom were suffering greatly from anxiety about their immediate families and were distressed at the thought of their families' struggle to cope or even survive in the prisoner's absence, particularly when they were regarded as a main breadwinner. Unpaid rent, loans, mortgages, medical fees and children's school or college fees were all of central concern.

In the context of gender, evidence shows that female prisoners from Africa and Asia face severe problems. For female prisoners, family rejection, worries about the effects of the inmate's imprisonment on the children, the family name and family status in society, concern about the family safety and anxiety about the health of some family members were predominant.

The issue of West African female drug couriers has been highlighted as being particularly serious for this group. When remanded in custody, they not only lose their freedom – they lose everything. Marriages break up, fathers disown their children and children reject their parents. Although other foreign prisoners, such as Asians and South Americans, also suffer from similar problems, the large number of West Africans make this group a major cause for concern and they have gradually become substantially over-represented in the current prison system.

Another important problem which deserves mention relates to the predicament faced by Nigerian children accompanying their mothers. Many of the Nigerian women who are sentenced for importation of drugs have one or two children with them. In some cases, they are pregnant. Whatever the case, the children are taken into care and newborn children only spend a few months with their mothers inside prison before being fostered. The grief of being separated from their children is compounded by the fact that children growing up in foster homes adopt the culture and lifestyle of their foster family and tend to grow away from their natural mothers. Meanwhile, the children left back home have to fend for themselves and if they survive, are frequently disturbed and traumatised. When a woman is reunited with her children after serving a long sentence, the mother and child relationship no longer exists and they are virtual strangers to one another.

Changing practice

There has been some improvement in practice and the prison service has extended the amount of time young children can stay with their mothers in some prisons. Furthermore, a children's visiting day has been introduced in HMP Holloway on a twice monthly basis, which allows the children to visit their mothers for the entire day.

In the context of West African women, the pioneering work carried out by AFAS (African Family Advisory Service), a project of Save The Children Fund, is worth mentioning. AFAS advised African families on Childcare law, day care provision and private fostering. In addition to providing advice to local authority social workers, AFAS focused on issues related to private fostering such as legislation. AFAS has been involved in social work training courses and had several times arranged for Nigerian social workers to visit the United Kingdom for further training.

By arranging international workshops and multi-professional visits, AFAS has built up a solid base for inter-country work between the United Kingdom and Nigeria which has had a significant impact on private fostering and child care issues. AFAS has also participated in many UK-based conferences and ran a workshop 'Developing Strategies to meet the Needs of Foreign women in UK Prisons' at a Home Office National Conference for governors of female prison establishments in 1992. The project has now ended.

Much of our original report was concerned with prison conditions themselves. The response here has been a mixed one. A frequently encountered comment on our proposals was that the prison conditions complained of were common to all prisoners – domestic as well as foreign as if there was nothing specific or special about the problems facing foreigners. This was of course to miss the point about the particular impact of bad conditions on prisoners who were both isolated and systematically disadvantaged in other ways. Clearly an improvement in overall prison conditions would have important benefits for foreign prisoners, but many other problems would still remain.

Within the prison, the lack of information, coupled with ignorance of the prison rules, can have a debilitating effect on foreign prisoners. Little effort has yet gone into systematically making translations and translators available. The uncertainty which is generated, along with isolation and lack of information, are the main problems foreign prisoners have to contend with. Communication problems also beset the foreign prisoners and it is important to recognise that translations of information will not necessarily be adequate for total understanding.

Cultural and religious differences can also impede an effective two-way communication process. There has been no systematic response to our call for cultural awareness training to assist staff in tackling these problems, although several workshop exercises have been undertaken and good training material for inter-agency work is available. A training initiative is important not least because of the impetus it can give to future work, as well as being a necessary part of improving the quality of existing services. A training pack should be developed which can be used by a range of trainers. Work on anti-racism and anti-discriminatory practice should precede training on cultural differences because of the way discrimination is intimately bound up with the treatment of foreign prisoners.

Our original report also proposed regional prisons which could concentrate in a specialist way on foreign prisoners. This seems to have happened informally, but too many prisoners are still isolated in small numbers in a range of ill equipped prisons. There is no doubt that suitable regimes can only really be developed in establishments with significant numbers of foreign prisoners, and we have been disappointed by the unwillingness of the Prison Department to implement our suggestion. There is no doubt that security allocation factors and a political concern about absconding foreign prisoners, has made it difficult to pursue this issue, but in our view, there has been too much caution. This has prevented many foreign prisoners suitable for open conditions, from actually getting to them.

As we have outlined, foreign prisoners, particularly drug couriers, face many problems which seem intractable. However, a number of encouraging initiatives have been taken over the past two years.

Further restrictions

The Criminal Justice Act 1991 was instrumental in ensuring that reports were prepared before imposition of a custodial sentence. The Middlesex Probation Service's Foreign Nationals Unit undertook valuable work producing reports, primarily on drug traffickers arrested at Heathrow Airport (see Abernethy and Hammond; and Hammond, this volume). The PSRs (pre-sentence reports) produced for foreign nationals offered some encouragement about the impact of reports on sentences as well as ensuring that the offender enters prison with an initial assessment of his/her circumstances. It is therefore very unfortunate that the Criminal Justice and Public Order Act 1994 removed the mandatory requirement for pre-sentence reports (see Hammond, this volume).

The approach to Discretionary Conditions Release (parole) is also confusing and unfair to foreign prisoners. For domestic prisoners serving sentences of over 4 years, much of the assessment work is based on risk assessment and assumes people will be supervised on release. Good quality risk assessment reports incorporating material from overseas agencies could be prepared, but supervision (or lack of it) remains an issue to be resolved for the foreign prisoner.

Home Leave/Temporary Release has become generally much more difficult to secure because of the current Home Office pre-occupation with security. The impact on foreign prisoners has been significant:

1. they now seem less likely to be located in open or semi-open conditions;

2. their chance of temporary release/home leave is even more limited; and

3. the tightening up of resources in both the prison and probation services limits further the potential for targeted work.

Prison and Probation Service initiatives

Over the past few years, the Prison and Probation Services have taken a number of initiatives. Some prisons have made real efforts, particularly those holding substantial numbers. In recent years, both probation and prison staff have recognised the value of voluntary sector input and have benefited from their cultural expertise. There has been a more concerted effort to involve outside organizations, who have been more than willing to respond to the needs of foreign prisoners.

A limited initiative taken by the Prison Service concerns permission for phone calls and provision of phone cards to prisoners. Unfortunately, this only highlights the problems of distance faced by foreign prisoners. A card used for a 10 minute conversation within the UK, is unlikely to last 2 minutes calling an overseas number many thousands of miles away. Some prisons have taken a positive stance regarding telephone calls and allow more frequent calls in lieu of visits. Unfortunately, there is no fixed norm and the degree to which prisons cater for foreign offenders' needs, varies significantly. As in many fields of policy, local flexibility may be attractive to managers but frequently also enables discriminatory practice. Telephone privileges have, however, now been withdrawn in the wake of the Woodcock Inquiry into prison security in 1995.

The identification of a clearer strategy in some probation services (eg. Inner London Probation Service) has helped trigger a more pro-active stance in certain prisons. Seconded probation teams in some London prisons have set up African and Spanish speaking support groups for foreign prisoners. These groups are held twice a month and 11 support groups have been set up with the co-operation of the prison staff.

The establishment of a Foreign Offenders' Good Practice Group set up by the ILPS prison probation division is another initiative. In addition to prison probation officers, representatives from outside agencies and embassies participate in the group meetings, which address issues of good practice and include exchange of infor- mation and experience on matters relating to foreign prisoners. A Resource Guide for people working with foreign offenders was published by ILPS in 1994 and there has been progress in develop- ing links with home countries (see Heaven; Abernethy and Ham- mond; and Hammond, this volume).[1]

Within Europe, more inter-agency cooperation is possible yet in some respects, progress has been much slower. The pre-occupation with drug enforcement policy issues is extremely frustrating, given the important immigration patterns and the ease of access. Many important health promotions and criminal justice issues have yet to be taken up within Europe.

Since our report, there have been a number of research initiatives and publications (summarised and footnoted throughout this volume) which have created a greater awareness of the problems and needs of foreign offenders and have provided recommenda- tions and guidelines for an improved service to this group.

Conclusion

There has been some progress and some acknowledgement of the need for further change. The issue of foreign prisoners will, it seems, continue to be an important one, involving many people's lives. As international inequality continues, it will continue to have a dimension in UK prisons, and it will continue to test our values and assumptions given the continuing association with such emotionally charged issues as drug trafficking. The location and shape of the problem will, however, change. It may not always be associated with West Africa and South America, and our own role should be to ensure a flexible response to the problems of a group whose difficulties in prison, regardless of variability, transcend national difference. The signs are, after all, that new drugs markets and new supply lines are developing and we may yet see drugs arriving from a dislocated and impoverished Eastern Europe. In the long run, it is important to realise that long prison sentences may not be the answer.

Note

1. There are two other helpful handbooks: *Immigration Detention*, Detention Advice Service 1995; and *Immigration and Deportation – Information Pack*, Nottinghamshire Probation Service 1994.

4
Working With Foreign National Offenders: A Role for the Probation Service

Rosemary Abernethy and Nick Hammond

Introduction

In September 1991, Middlesex Probation Service (MPS) established a pilot project to work with foreign nationals arrested at Heathrow Airport for drug importation offences. MPS was concerned about this group of defendants, covering as it does both Uxbridge Magistrates Court, where those arrested at Heathrow Airport first appear, and also Isleworth Crown Court to which the majority of Customs cases are committed for trial. This project was to be 'action research' and its general remit was to address the question of what the probation service could do, pre-sentence, in working with foreign national drug importers.

A principal objective of the pilot project was to test the feasibility of preparing pre-sentence reports on foreign nationals, not normally resident in the UK, who are arrested for drug importation offences. Prior to the establishment of this pioneering project, social enquiry reports (from October 1992 pre-sentence reports (PSRs)) were not generally prepared by the probation service on defendants who did not have an address in the UK and there was no experience or body of knowledge within the probation service in this country on preparing court reports on this group of defendants. Questions such as 'What would be the similarities and the differences in preparing reports on foreign nationals and residents be compared with British nationals?' would need to be addressed.

Would it be a matter of transferring existing probation skills in report writing or developing new methods of working combined with additional knowledge and expertise? Would foreign nationals cooperate in the preparation of these reports and would they consent to corroborated information being obtained from their home country?

The second principal purpose of the project was to delineate those services which MPS might provide, or obtain, for those foreign nationals arrested whilst awaiting trial. The results and lessons learnt from this project, while informing MPS' own policy on working with foreign nationals would, it was hoped, also have a wider influence on the work and practice of other probation services. This was therefore an important research project in terms of its potential contribution to probation practice. The project was concluded in October 1992 when MPS published *Drug Couriers: a role for the probation service*.

In summary, it was found feasible to prepare full, realistic and useful reports for the courts. In some circumstances, it was possible to obtain information from defendants' home countries in order to verify information contained in the reports. It was concluded that the skills of probation officers were readily transferable to the provision of reports on this group of defendants. The views of sentencers, gauged both from public statements in the court room and from private interviews, indicated that reports were felt to be relevant, realistic and useful. They were also helpful to prison staff in sentence planning and post sentence work. Services developed during the life of the pilot project included provision of information to prison probation and education departments, early notification to prison reception staff of language, health and other welfare issues and the encouragement of voluntary organisations in their work with foreign national prisoners.

Following the implementation of the Criminal Justice Act 1991 in October 1992, MPS decided to continue the project and changed its name to the Foreign Nationals Unit. The Unit's two probation officers now have over four years experience of working exclusively with foreign nationals arrested at Heathrow Airport and in preparing PSRs for Crown Court. Given that Heathrow is the largest single entry point for foreign nationals arrested in the UK, the Unit's probation officers have unique experience and opportunities to develop probation practice in working with foreign nationals who have no address, and frequently no contacts, in this country. What follows is a summary of the Unit's work with foreign nationals, contact at court, preparation of PSRs and other development work.

Customs arrests at Heathrow Airport

During the operation of the project, approximately three hundred people were arrested annually, at Heathrow by the Customs and Excise Service, for drug offences. (This does not include the larger number of people given 'on the spot' fines for possession of a small quantity of a Class B drug who never attend court.) Those arrested are either given police bail or kept in custody to appear at the earliest opportunity at Uxbridge Magistrates Court. In most years approximately one-third of this total will be UK residents, most of whom are UK nationals, with the remaining two-thirds being non-UK residents, principally foreign nationals.

The profile of those foreign nationals arrested at Heathrow varies from year to year, reflecting as it does the targeting priorities and arrests of the Customs Service, the changing pattern of international drug trafficking and the scheduling policy of the British Airports Authority and individual airlines. Nevertheless, it is possible to make some generalizations. In recent years, the majority of foreign nationals arrested at Heathrow have been either from the source countries in South America and Asia or from transit countries in West Africa or North America. In comparison, foreign nationals arrested at Gatwick Airport are primarily from the Caribbean, reflecting the schedule and charter flights into that airport. Customs arrests at the south coast ports are predominately of European nationals.

While UK and non-UK nationals are 'processed' through the same criminal justice system, their individual experiences will be dependant upon their fluency in English and their ability to communicate with those about them, their particular knowledge of the British court and prison system, their cultural beliefs and values and the presence of friends or family in this country. While these factors can also have an influence on UK residents and nationals, they are more likely to acutely affect non-UK nationals and residents.

The majority of drug couriers are arrested following long inter-continental flights when they are tired and 'jet-lagged'. After their arrest and questioning by Customs Officers, they are brought to Uxbridge Magistrates Court either later the same day or the fol-lowing day. If the means of concealment of drugs was internal ('stuffers' or 'swallowers' in Customs parlance), warrants for exten-sion of detention will be obtained from the court until the courier has 'gone clear'. The average weight of drugs concealed in this way (in condoms or in the fingers of surgical gloves) is around 300 grams, although it can be considerably more. This means of concealment will be confirmed by Customs Officers after taking a urine sample and testing for opiates. The courier will be X-rayed at hospital by consent, or detained until Customs' suspicions are either confirmed or proved groundless. There have been several cases since September 1991 when the courier was detained in hospital due to medical complications caused by leakage from the packages of drugs. In the autumn of 1992 there were several deaths caused by this means of concealment.

A small number of couriers (both UK and non-UK residents) who are arrested carrying small quantities of cannabis (more occasionally heroin or cocaine) are given Police bail from Heath-row Police Station and given a date to appear at Uxbridge Magis-trates Court. However, the majority of those arrested are brought to court in custody from the holding cells at Heathrow Police Station. Many arrested foreign nationals will have been allowed by Customs to make a phone call home to inform family or friends of their arrest and detention. This is more likely to have been allowed when the defendant has been cooperative with Customs investigations and when such contact would not compromise any additional investigations in the defendant's home country or in the UK.

The Unit Probation Officer on duty that day approaches the Customs Court Liaison Officer and obtains details of new arrests: the nature of the charge, type and approximate weight of the drug, method of concealment, country of residence and nationality, command of English, whether there were any children accompany-ing the detainee, the position of any children left at home, any medical conditions known, mental health or drug abuse problems and the name of the solicitor. If available, the investigating Customs Officer will be asked to comment on how the defendant presented in interview, whether s/he was cooperative, and/or was allowed any contact with home.

Before seeing the defendant, the Unit POs seek background information from the defendant's solicitor including details of any previous trips to the UK, family circumstances, the possibility of bail and availability of sureties. In some cases, the solicitor, who might also have been up half the previous night with the client during Customs interviews, will know the situation well. In others, the solicitor may have only been called in that morning and know little about the defendant. Solicitors have readily accepted that the Unit's work can provide a valuable service to their clients and assist them in coping with their remand in custody and related problems.

Primarily, the Unit's first interview with the foreign national defendant in the cells is to assess and identify immediate needs and welfare problems and to provide information to assist in coping with admission to a 'foreign' prison. An initial problem is how to introduce yourself to a foreign national defendant. In many countries, there is no such organisation as the probation service and even in those countries where one does exist, the roles, responsibilities and ethics of that service may differ widely. Introductions are frequently made by the solicitor who assures the defendant that probation officers are independent of Customs or the Immigration Service and that they are there to assist them and give them useful information. The PO then briefly explains our role. A defendant rarely remains suspicious and unreceptive throughout an initial interview.

Most non-UK resident suspects have never been to prison in their own country, let alone in the UK. They are frequently confused, disorientated and frightened by detention in this country. Many of them experience a culture shock which is especially acute during the first few days. Foreign nationals' expectations of the criminal justice system, police, Customs, prisons and probation officers are usually based upon their knowledge and opinions of similar agencies in their own country. Many fear violence and intimidation in the prison system and assume the criminal justice system is corrupt. When asked by a probation officer whether Customs had released any money (confiscated from the defendant at the time of arrest) for use whilst on remand, one West African man assumed that a bribe was being requested.

Initial questions of foreign nationals being interviewed in the court cells on their first appearance concentrate on their immediate well-being, such as whether they have eaten or have any medical problems. These early exchanges let the suspects know that the service is concerned about them and their welfare and enable an assessment of how much information they can absorb and understand. In a state of anxiety and apprehension, in an unfamiliar country and setting, it is difficult for anyone to absorb more than a limited amount of information. Such information has to be clear, kept to a minimum, simplified and repeated when necessary.

Defendants are asked if they have been able to inform their families back home of their detention. Even though Customs can allow phone calls to be made soon after arrest, couriers frequently will not have informed families that they were travelling outside the country. Defendants are told of their entitlements to letters whilst on remand and the possibility, though expensive and difficult, of telephoning abroad. Solicitors and probation officers are sometimes asked to contact families but in the main, foreign nationals say they will write from prison themselves.

The initial interview in the cells at magistrates court is therefore designed to make an accurate assessment of the defendant's ability to cope in prison and identify any immediate welfare problems. Defendants are informed, verbally and in writing, about the prison regime, the reception process and access to medical services, chaplaincy and prison probation officers. Prison authorities can be alerted to any immediate issues by a form drawn up by the Unit accompanying the defendant to prison. This has proved of particular benefit to non-English speakers. The Unit also provides the defendant with a copy of a local information sheet, written in cooperation with the two remand prisons serving the Court – Holloway and Wormwood Scrubs. This short pamphlet is available in English and Spanish and is regularly updated. On arrival at prison, foreign national prisoners should be provided by the reception staff with their own copy of two joint Prison Service and Prison Reform Trust publications (available in 14 languages), the Prisoners' Information Pack and the Foreign Prisoners' Resource Pack. The Unit will supply them should the prison not do so.

Foreign nationals frequently misunderstand what they are told by lawyers or are given little or no information. It is therefore important to explain the nature of the court process and legal language, and after the hearing, to find out if they have understood what has happened to them. For example, 'jurisdiction declined', 'target date for committal', 'Section 6:1 and 6:2s' are bewildering terms which contribute little to an understanding of what is happening. The Unit also advises clients on the time their case will take to reach trial at Crown Court.

If the relevant bi-lateral agreement has been signed, the Police and Criminal Evidence Act 1984 requires Customs officers to notify the arrested person's consulate or High Commission of his/her detention, whether or not s/he wishes it. From our experience, it is not safe to assume that a foreign national's consulate or High Commission will be aware of their national's detention even if the country is signatory to the convention. Even if the consulate is informed, they will not necessarily initiate contact on receipt of the name. With certain exceptions, such as the American and Dutch who automatically arrange visits, it is necessary for the defendant or someone acting on his/her behalf (for example the Unit) to request contact. The desire of foreign nationals to have contact with their embassy varies widely and cannot be generalised simply on the basis of which embassy it is or whether the defendant is pleading guilty or not guilty, although these factors are all relevant. The majority of Colombian nationals (not a signatory to the convention) request contact with their consulate despite the nature of their plea. However, the majority of Nigerian defendants (whose Government is a signatory) expressly do not wish to have contact with their high commission. The principal reason given is they are fearful that their family back home will be harassed by the Nigerian authorities and that contact will increase the likelihood of being re-sentenced under Decree 33[1] on their eventual return.

Defendants are also given the opportunity of being put in contact with a range of voluntary groups working with foreign national prisoners. Foreign nationals may not be so reluctant to confide in voluntary workers as they are with their embassy or others in authority within the prison.

There are several groups working with women in Holloway Prison which have established credibility and a good working relationship with prison staff, including the prison probation service. The Unit has contact with the African Prisoners' Scheme (APS), the Female Prisoners Welfare Unit and its related organization, Hibiscus. The APS runs a support group in the education department and the valuable work of the FPWP and Hibiscus in re-establishing contact between prisoners and their families in Nigeria and Jamaica is discussed elsewhere in this volume. The Unit has regular contact with Group Amigo who assist Spanish-speaking (mainly Colombian) prisoners whose lack of English and distance from home creates particular problems. Foreign national defendants may come across these groups by other means but the Unit tries to ensure that no-one is neglected.

Male foreign prisoners have access to very few support groups. Two voluntary groups, Fujaltu and Group Vamos Juntos, perform a befriending role for African and Spanish speaking men and a Spanish speakers' group and an African men's group have been established at Wormwood Scrubs Prison. The groups are run by probation officers and volunteers and frequently have guests from consulates and other voluntary agencies.

Preparation of pre-sentence reports on foreign national defendants

A discussion about the pre-sentence report is held with the defendant and the defendant's solicitor at the earliest appropriate time. Normally, the probation service does not enquire about a defendant's plea until the committal hearing but with foreign national defendants, information is sought from solicitors at an earlier stage to provide the Unit with sufficient time to make enquiries abroad. The pre-sentence report is usually prepared by the Unit PO who first saw the defendant during court duty. The PO will have had the benefit of seeing the defendant regularly but interviews at prison specifically to collect information for the report will only occur when the defendant and the solicitor have confirmed that a guilty plea will be entered.

Information concerning the offence, including a prosecution statement and a summary of the case, is provided by the Customs and Excise Service's Solicitors Department. Police antecedents and previous criminal convictions (if known) will be available from the police. It is not good practice to rely solely upon the defendant's account of the offence when discussing involvement and culpability.

The prosecution should have details of any previous convictions for UK nationals and residents by the time of the committal. The situation is more problematic for non-UK nationals/residents. It is the responsibility of the Heathrow Airport police (where all Customs charges are formally laid) to obtain information on previous criminal convictions and to prepare antecedent histories. Although it is unusual for a foreign national, not usually resident in the country, to have any recorded convictions in the UK, there have been small number who have served previous prison sentences in the UK for drug trafficking offences.

It is also rare for the records of previous convictions from abroad to be available to the court or report writer. It is extremely difficult, if not impossible, to obtain previous criminal records from some countries – including many countries in Europe. Customs officials remain sceptical about whether reliable information can be obtained, especially given that couriers often travel on false documents, but will pursue such information if the defendant is suspected of having previous convictions. In the vast majority of cases, the police antecedents state 'no criminal convictions recorded in the UK' and the Court assumes the defendant is a first time offender.

The prosecution depositions indicate the defendant's initial reactions to detention and arrest; whether there was a sophisticated or well rehearsed cover story; how the defendant first came to the notice of Customs, including demeanour and response to Custom's enquiries; and the degree of co-operation given to Customs. It is estimated that approximately 80 percent of couriers are identified 'cold' by customs officers using judgments based on passenger profiles. Couriers are also stopped as a result of information forwarded by ticket agents, airline staff and cabin crews or from Customs enquiries and intelligence.

Information from depositions can contribute to the probation assessment of the courier's role in the importation, including whether the courier was part of a larger organization, recruited and prepared by an established drug trafficking network or a small scale entrepreneur. There may be limited information in the depositions about the degree of co-operation given to Customs but Customs officers and prosecution counsel will inform the judge privately in chambers when a defendant has given substantial assistance. The probation officer and the PSR writer will not enquire about the extent of co-operation unless the defendant chooses to raise the subject.

It is necessary to compare the defendant's description of the offence with that provided by the prosecution and to assess the reasons for any discrepancies. The defendant's explanation and motivation for committing the offence will be discussed at length, as will his/her background, personal and family circumstances and work record.

Corroboration from abroad

When a guilty plea is confirmed, the defendant is asked whether s/he consents to enquiries about personal circumstances being made in his/her home country. Such enquiries provide the court with otherwise unavailable information which may corroborate the defendant's evidence. Foreign nationals commonly complain that their sentencing court had no interest in hearing about their background or reasons for the offence.[2] Some judges may feel that current sentencing guidelines make such information inappropriate, especially given Lord Lane's view in *Aramah*, that when sentencing for drug trafficking offences, there will be few, if any, occasions when anything other than an immediate custodial sentence is considered and that good character and/or compelling personal circumstances are of less importance than in other types of case.[3] Nevertheless, verification of a foreign national defendant's background gives greater credibility to mitigation and the PSR can counter inaccurate stereotypes.

These issues are carefully discussed with the defendant whose informed consent is required for any enquiries. Depending on the country, we will discuss which agency we will use to make enquiries; the response we have had to previous enquiries; the status of the person who would undertake the home visit (eg. voluntary aid worker, social worker, probation officer, government official); what questions will be asked; issues of confidentiality and how the PSR writer will use any information obtained.

The majority of foreign nationals on whom PSRs are prepared consent to enquiries being made in their own countries. The Unit has developed a network of contacts to obtain independent information from abroad, particularly international agencies such as the Red Cross, International Social Services; embassies – mainly the American and Colombian; and voluntary organizations with links abroad such as FPWP and Hibiscus.

The safety of their families is the most important factor considered by defendants when deciding whether to consent. If they believe that enquiries would place family members at risk of repercussions or harassment, they are highly unlikely to agree to them being undertaken. As noted above, this particularly applies to Nigerians, some of whom are willing to have their families visited by non-governmental organizations like Hibiscus. Nevertheless, it has proved possible to obtain home circumstances reports in over a third of PSRs written by the Unit. In a further quarter of cases, consent was given but there was insufficient time for information to be obtained.

International comparisons

Nigeria

In contrast to the gender division for all foreign nationals arrested at Heathrow (72 percent male; 28 percent female) the profile of Nigerian couriers shows that men and women are equally represented. Drug couriers cited general background economic hardship exacerbated by recent unemployment, bereavement of a breadwinner or illness as the most frequent stated motivation behind the offence. Female couriers almost uniformly described being recruited by a drug organiser in Nigeria and being paid a fixed sum for the successful completion of the importation. The majority of female couriers stated they were market traders and had travelled to the UK previously for purchasing trips.

Male Nigerian couriers generally are better educated, often graduates and professionals, and frequently described themselves as small entrepreneurial businessmen, experiencing severe financial problems since the government's economic structural adjustment programme of the mid 1980s (see Joshua in this volume). Amongst the male couriers there was evidence that they took a more active role in the organization of the importation and would realise a larger share of the profits, rather than being a 'simple' courier paid a flat rate for their involvement.

Ghana
Ghanaian nationals comprise the second largest nationality group (excluding UK nationals) after Nigerian citizens seen at the Unit. Verified home background information can be received from Ghana via the International Red Cross or International Social Services.

Colombia
Colombians (regardless of their intended plea at court) rarely display the reluctance shown by other nationalities to having contact with their consular officials and virtually all of them requested visits. Similarly, most wish to have home enquiries made through the government welfare agency, Bienestar Familiar. Such report requests are sent directly to the Colombian Consulate for translation and onward referral to Colombia.

Some brief observations on Colombian couriers as a group may be made. There were eight times more men than women and the Colombian couriers appeared to be more from the 'classic courier stereotype', coming from the rural and urban poor, recruited solely for a one-off payment on the successful completion of the importation. Many of the men had experience in the Army beyond their military service which appears to be a significant factor in recruitment. The men cited long term unemployment and poverty as their reasons for becoming couriers. Amongst this group, there was considerable fear that assisting the Customs Service with information might lead to possible repercussions for their families in Colombia. There have been several cases of Colombians pleading not guilty to their offence, with a defence of duress, despite the drugs having been internally concealed. A significant proportion of the male couriers were well educated, to degree level, and had 'professional' occupations in the law and journalism before more recent periods of unemployment.

United States
US citizens are fortunate in receiving a high standard of consular services from their embassy. Most of the American defendants on whom reports have been prepared have been content for enquiries to be made into their home circumstances. The Unit, in conjunction with the US Embassy, has developed a successful procedure

for obtaining home circumstances reports from the US Probation Service.

Pakistan

Some Pakistani nationals have agreed to enquiries being made of their families in their homes through the Red Crescent Society assisted by the International Division of the Red Cross in London. A larger, more detailed, consent form with more specific questions attached was devised for these enquiries, given that these are made by local field officers in Pakistan and not by trained social workers. Reports have been received in good time for the court hearing.

Turkey

Most Turkish nationals seen to date have not wanted visits or contact with their Embassy, their only explanation being that they believed they could be re-sentenced on returning to Turkey for a drug related offence and do not want to draw unnecessary attention to themselves. A Turkish national on whom a report was written agreed for enquiries to be made by the Turkish Red Crescent Society. A basic report confirming his family circumstances and the family's problems due to his arrest was received prior to his trial and the report was presented in its entirety.

Bolivia

The Bolivian Consul in London provides very limited services following a 1988 Government decree forbidding Consular services to convicted drug importers. However, good quality reports have been written by social workers from a Catholic social work mission in Bolivia and obtained via International Social Services. The social workers offer additional support to the couriers' families in Bolivia after the court case.

Canada

Reports on Canadians have been obtained from a social welfare agency as well as the government Social Security Department via the International Social Services. These reports were prepared by qualified Canadian social workers to a highly professional standard and were submitted in their entirety to the Crown Court.

Holland

Dutch nationals in UK prisons benefit during their sentence from the support of a network of voluntary visitors established and supported by their consulate. The scheme is comprehensive, efficient and highly valued by Dutch nationals. Home circumstances reports on Dutch citizens can also be obtained via a specialist probation unit in the Netherlands.

Italy

Limited reports on Italian nationals can be sought via the Italian Consulate with whom the project has established a procedure to obtain information.

Spain

Information from Spain has been sent and obtained via the Spanish Consulate in London and the ISS who approached the relevant local authority welfare services in Spain.

Summary

Given the complexities involved, writing a PSR on a foreign national is a lengthy procedure usually taking longer than for other categories of offenders. It is often necessary to clarify information received from other agencies and it is always valuable for the report writer to do some initial research into the defendant's home country.

Since the implementation of the Criminal Justice Act 1991 in October 1992, the Crown Court at Isleworth has had available pre-sentence reports on foreign nationals who plead or are found guilty, after trial. The Judges have indicated in comments during sentencing that they have found these reports of use and benefit. Defence barristers make reference to their contents when arguing for mitigation. Defendants now have the opportunity to have their own explanation and description of the offence, their background, and present personal circumstances available in a probation pre-sentence report. It is premature to assess the influence such reports have on sentencing patterns. Illegal importation of drugs inevitably results in a substantial custodial sentence. Nonetheless, the provision of pre-sentence reports is contributing towards greater understanding of foreign national defendants appearing before courts in this country and providing for a greater understanding of the background and motivation of drug smuggling.

Notes

1. Decree, or Edict 33, was issued in 1990 and states that any Nigerian citizen arrested/charged or convicted for a drug related offence which originated in Nigeria on or after 10 October 1990, would on their return be charged with a new offence and liable to a prison sentence of 5 years.
2. Penny Green, *Drug Couriers*, Howard League for Penal Reform, July 1991; Tarzi, A. and Hedge, J., *A Prison Within a Prison – a Study of Foreign Offenders*, Inner London Probation Service, 1990.
3. (1982) 76 Cr App R 190; see also the discussions of this case in Part One of this volume.

5
Turning Back the Clock: The Implications for Pre-sentence Reports of the Criminal Justice and Public Order Act 1994

Nick Hammond[1]

Introduction

The Criminal Justice & Public Order Act 1994 (CJPOA) could have significant implications for the way in which foreign national defendants, amongst other minority groups within the criminal justice system, are sentenced. The Criminal Justice Act 1991 required courts to consider pre-sentence reports (PSRs) before imposing a custodial sentence on all offences except those which can only be tried on indictment. Most Customs evasion offences (except conspiracy cases) come into this category and it was due to this legal requirement that probation services provided PSRs.

Schedule 9, para 40 of the CJPOA restores to the courts the power to make a custodial sentence without having a PSR. This has particular implications for those being sentenced for drug trafficking offences (both UK and non-Uk residents) where substantial prison sentences are usually made.

My research carried out in 1994 sought to examine the value, impact and effectiveness of PSRs prepared on foreign national drug couriers. Of major concern, was the potential impact of the new legislation and whether judges would revert to the pre 1991 Act situation. The implementation of the relevant section of the 1994 Act in February 1995 heightened the importance of the research, since it could record the impact of PSRs on a group of offenders who may not continue to have reports prepared comprehensively in the future.

The aim was to take a 'snapshot' of the views and opinions of those who have reports prepared on them and those who use them in their work – from Crown Court judges and barristers, prison probation and prison officers to sentenced foreign national prisoners themselves. Over 74 interviews were conducted in the Autumn of 1994. These included interviews with judges from the two Crown Court centres which deal with the majority of drug traffickers from Heathrow and Gatwick Airports – Isleworth and Croydon – as well as defence advocates who represent couriers. Six prisons were also visited (two female and four male establishments) where interviews were carried out with prison probation officers and prison staff as well as 24 sentenced foreign nationals (seven women and seventeen men).

The full report, *The Value of Pre-Sentence Reports on Foreign Nationals*, was published by Middlesex Probation Service in 1995. A short summary of the main findings has relevance to how court practice may be affected by the 1994 Act and the implications for non-UK foreign national drug couriers and those within the criminal justice system who work with them.

Prompted by the mandatory requirement for PSRs in the 1991 Act the Middlesex Probation Service established the Foreign Nationals Unit (see Abernethy and Hammond in this volume) and probation services with a similar interest in this group of offenders have shared their developing knowledge and expertise at quarterly meetings of practitioners. Contacts have been developed with voluntary groups, embassies, high commissions and international organizations to improve services for detained foreign nationals and networks established to obtain corroborated information from abroad. A biannual 'Good Practice Forum' bringing together prison probation officers, prison officers and voluntary organizations to discuss a variety of practical issues of concern to those within the criminal justice system working with this group of prisoners has been hosted by Middlesex since 1992. Workshops have been arranged by the Foreign Nationals Unit for the welfare staff from embassies and high commissions to examine and improve the services provided for their imprisoned nationals. Partnership funding has also been found for voluntary organizations specialising in working with this group of prisoners.

Probation officers preparing PSRs for the Crown Court on defendants facing sentences for Customs offences have always been very aware of the limitations of PSRs given the inevitability of a substantial custodial sentence for the importation of a Class A drug. Nevertheless, such PSRs are subject to national standards and the usual gate-keeping and monitoring procedures established within probation offices and at Crown Court to provide 'quality control'. Good quality reports on foreign national couriers go against the general direction of reports in the probation service because of the importance of including ethnicity and family background information when settling the offence in context. The usual monitoring mechanisms ensure that report writers do not employ racial and gender stereotypes.

Judges' views of PSRs for foreign national offenders

There was a consensus that the probation service provides PSRs of a good standard on this group of defendants. There were favourable comments on the quality of many reports and the commitment to obtaining corroborated information from people's home countries:

> The quality of the reports are really very good, generally speaking it is higher than the general quality of other reports. . . .

> I'm really amazed at your ingenuity to get all this information from countries where English isn't their spoken language.

Judges were, however, critical of the value and necessity of PSRs in the sentencing process where custody is inevitable, as it is in all but exceptional drug importation cases (usually only those involving a relatively minor amount of class B drugs). Judges felt that background information coming from the same source (the defendant), with infrequent opportunities to verify its authenticity, could as readily be placed before them by the defence. It was said that whether information came from the defence or the probation service, its influence on sentence length would be marginal when tariff sentencing was operating. Some judges acknowledged that the preparation of the PSR could be a significant contribution to the defendant's sense that s/he had been treated fairly and justly.

It was acknowledged that PSRs could have a valuable role post-sentence as an assessment for through-care work by prison probation officers and prison staff. Judges were looking forward to the return of their discretion in requesting PSRs rather than having to accept them as mandatory. Nonetheless, if probation services continued to provide PSRs on a pre-hearing basis on guilty pleas without the court adjourning for them, judges indicated that they would continue to read them. However, few judges could foresee occasions when they would adjourn the hearing specifically for the production of a PSR, after conviction or a late plea.

Judges stated that defence counsel would need to convince them of the grounds for an adjournment and while 'age and health' considerations were cited as possible acceptable reasons, the over-all impression was that the counsel would have to make a very persuasive case. Judges acknowledged that there were increasing pressures on courts to progress cases speedily, without unnecessary delays, and that adjournments for PSRs for this type of offence would be unnecessary in the future.

One opinion was that the requirement for PSRs on offences such as drug importation was an unintended anomaly of the 1991 CJA:

... like so much in the 1991 CJA, I don't think that it was properly thought through. I don't think that it was ever envisaged that persons who came from remote parts of the world, from the depths of Colombia or Pakistan or Nigeria, would have to have probation reports prepared about them. I think that the probation service were confronted with a difficult situation and have done, in the circumstances, a very great deal. ...

When it is made mandatory (to have a PSR) as it is here, then undoubtedly you get anomalies.

Not all judges viewed changes in the Act favourably:

Well, I'm happy with the current situation, I'm happy to have PSRs all the time. I'm happy to have a PSR in every case because I think that there are times when, if you have the discretion, you won't ask for them, but if you had the report you might get to know something which you hadn't known. I'm quite happy with the statutory provision of PSRs as it is . . .

If the law changes, I think that it's retrograde, I would have preferred it to stay the way it is.

What lawyers think

Those barristers and solicitors interviewed described a sense of frustration at the limited scope for mitigation in drug importation offences. No other offence is dependent to such an extent on a sentencing tariff and it is this, combined with an element of deterrent sentencing, that legal representatives felt restricted their scope for mitigation:

The guidelines to sentencing are such that it doesn't matter what you say.

Similarly, barristers and solicitors felt that the value of PSRs in affecting sentencing lengths was marginal. Solicitors in particular found difficulty in appreciating that probation officers, when preparing PSRs, had a different role and focus compared to themselves. Some felt that their work was being duplicated. However, solicitors (more than barristers) thought that the attention given and work done with foreign nationals during the pre-trial process was of importance and they were more likely to view the provision of reports as contributing to their client's sense of being treated as an individual rather than a 'name and drug weight'.

Barristers varied in their enthusiasm for mitigation in such cases; some seemed to adapt a 'tariff mentality' which would affect the force of their mitigation. A few said they used the PSR to structure their mitigation, to 'hang' points on, and in that regard it was of value. Looking towards the implementation of the PSR provisions in the CJPOA, barristers generally felt that it would lead to fewer reports being presented to the court for this offence as well as for other offences which were not borderline custody/community sentences. They also foresaw variations between judges:

> I can see that in some courts it will be wholly exceptional to see a PSR for this offence. . . .

> I suspect that a number of judges will say that in the usual case (of drug importation) there's no need for a report or will not be a need. My fear is that once it is no longer required by law to have one, every case will become the usual case. . . .

Barristers said they would continue to use PSRs if they were available, and hoped that judges would consider applications from them for an adjournment for a PSR, after conviction or late plea.

Probation officers in prisons

Prison probation officers were the most positive in their support for PSRs in their work with foreign national prisoners. At remand prisons, contact with a foreign national at an early stage by the field probation officer alerted them to problems and through-care issues which could be dealt with jointly. Conscious that the particular problems experienced by foreign nationals could be overlooked in a busy remand wing, early identification and joint work carried out in conjunction with the field probation officer, was valued. It was felt that the PSR formed an essential document for the probation team to use in sentence planning, offending behaviour work and discretionary release reports.

At the prisons holding foreign nationals after sentence and categorization, the PSR is frequently the sole information prison probation officers have during the induction interview or subsequent contact. PSRs and any associated casework assessment appear particularly useful when the prisoner's use of English is poor or non-existent. It is common knowledge that probation teams' contribution to sentence planning varies between establishments but where teams do contribute to sentence planning, PSRs are useful.

Prison probation officers felt that their work with this group of prisoners had benefited from the provision of PSRs and that the absence of them, for this group in particular, would further disadvantage a group already prone to being marginalized or discounted within the prison system:

PSRs are quite crucial in work done here. A good quality report would have a good analysis of the offence and the circumstances leading to it and that's something I can use in my work with the prisoner.

Probation officers valued the work undertaken and information obtained by the PSR writer about foreign national families abroad. They were concerned at the effect the possible loss of background work and pre-trial support sustained by PSRs would have on this group of defendants:

My general feeling is that it would be a seriously retrograde step and I feel it would be pretty disastrous. . . .

The absence of PSRs would significantly marginalise foreign nationals more so than UK residents. So they will experience discrimination which we have been trying hard to get rid of. A lot of recent effort, time and resources have gone into trying to provide a service which is reasonably equal for foreign nationals at the sentencing stage. They will experience that discrimination yet again. . . .

Prison officers' response

Prison staff usually first come across PSRs in the Observation, Categorization and Assessment Unit (OCA) or in their role as personal officers at the local prisons. OCA officers commented that PSRs are important when completing the initial stages of sentence planning. Prison officers usually have PSRs available to them at subsequent stages in sentence planning and for any throughcare issues brought to them by the foreign national prisoner. Officers felt that information in the PSR and any associated assessment from the report writer helped them understand the background and motivation of foreign national prisoners who will frequently come from an unfamiliar country and culture:

It is obviously a lot easier to do sentence planning if we have a report because it gives us an awful lot of information about a person's background, the circumstances of the offence, about

his attitudes and feelings which you often can't get; you have
time to sit down and talk with these people and they're possibly
more forthcoming to you [probation officer] than they are to
prison officers anyway.

Views of sentenced foreign nationals

Sentenced foreign nationals generally knew that the court would
sentence them according to the value of the drug they were carrying, their plea and their degree of cooperation with the Customs
service and that a very limited discount may be given due to their
family and personal circumstances. They were told this by their
legal representatives, prison probation officer, PSR writer as well
as by other prisoners. However, those interviewed were confused
by the sentencing practice and quoted wide variations in sentence
length for similar values of imported drugs. They attributed such
discrepancies to the judge taking mitigating circumstances into
account in other cases but not theirs, or to different sentencing
tariffs adopted by individual judges.

Nevertheless, foreign nationals were generally pleased that a
report had been prepared, that someone had listened to them and
that the court had the information available. They valued the
support, information and assistance with practical problems and
issues regarding their families at home, given them, pre-sentence,
by the report writer. Liaison probation officers at Crown Court
felt that PSRs had changed the attitude of foreign national
offenders post-sentence. There were fewer complaints about the
court process and a greater understanding of what was to happen
next. It was also observed that barristers use the PSR and that
the quality and commitment put into mitigation seemed to have
improved.

Conclusion

Unless the probation service continues to provide 'pre-hearing'
PSRs, it seems unlikely that courts will adjourn sentencing
specifically for their preparation. After the implementation of the
new Act it is likely that a large proportion of foreign national

prisoners will start their sentence without a PSR having been prepared. The advances and improvements to working practices made by the probation service in relation to this group of prisoners could be adversely affected if PSRs are no longer mandatory.

As a group, foreign national offenders face exceptional difficulties within the criminal justice system. The value of PSRs, if measured purely in terms of their impact on sentencing, would possibly justify abandonment. However, criminal justice should not be 'Treasury led'. All defendants need to see and feel that justice has been done and the provision of a PSR made a contribution to this perception. The probation service should argue that this group of prisoners is one experiencing unique difficulties with which they assist. It is to be hoped that when probation services develop their protocol with Crown Courts in the light of the CJPOA and the provision of PSRs, foreign nationals will not be discounted and disregarded.

Note

1. This research was made possible by a University of Cambridge Institute of Criminology Cropwood Fellowship awarded to Nick Hammond in 1994. This article should be read as a postscript to the article by Rosemary Abernethy and Nick Hammond in this volume.

6
Hibiscus: Working with Nigerian Women Prisoners

Olga Heaven

Introduction

Hibiscus was established in 1991 to assist Nigerian and Jamaican women under the umbrella of the Female Prisoners Welfare Project (FPWP) which provides support for black women in prison throughout the United Kingdom.

Black women constitute a prison population disproportionate to their numbers in the general population. The reasons for this are to be found in the economic, political and cultural make-up of society, as are the differences in treatment they experience once in prison.

The problems are multiplied for foreign prisoners, especially when they are involved in particularly unattractive and socially dangerous activities such as the importation of Class A drugs (chiefly cocaine or heroin). In addition to the normal factors which render their cases problematic, there are the issues of language difference, lack of information about their social and family circumstances and their history of offending in their home countries. Many of them are coming to this country for the first time and in most cases have never travelled out of their own countries before. Many are frightened and disoriented because of the unfamiliar environment and because of the discomfort and danger to their health and dignity, associated with the methods commonly used for concealing the drugs, such as swallowing condoms or plastic bags or concealing them in their genitalia.

The women are questioned, searched and arrested in shameful and often degrading circumstances. They are almost without exception held on remand, as bail is unlikely to be granted for the majority of foreign nationals who will in most cases be deported at the end of their sentences (see Stanley, this volume).

Our own research within Hibiscus shows that the average sentence per offender, most of whom were first offenders, between 1989 and 1992, was 6 years. While sentences (until recently), in the absence of background information relating to home circumstances and other mitigating factors, were supposed to be related to the 'street value' of the drugs, based on quantity and purity, this varies widely in practice. For attempting to import 400 grammes of cocaine, 'Alice' received a sentence of $7\frac{1}{2}$ years, while Mary Z received only $3\frac{1}{2}$ years sentence for attempting to import the same quantity of drugs. For attempting to import one kilogramme of cocaine (valued at £80,000), I.O. was given 6 years, while S.A. received $6\frac{1}{2}$ years for 200 grammes of cocaine, valued by Customs at £12,000.[1]

Since the majority of these women have children and most in our experience are single parents, the impact on their families left behind without care or support is devastating. Nigeria, from which a disproportionate number of these women come, is undergoing a severe economic crisis, has a very rudimentary system of social security, poor communications and a corrupt bureaucracy which rewards dishonesty rather than integrity and hard work. While these women might be considered 'criminals' in conventional terms, examination of their personal circumstances and social backgrounds shows that they are also victims.

Hibiscus was therefore set up in 1991 to alleviate some of the particularly severe problems that Nigerian women experience in British prisons. An office has been established in Lagos and is functioning smoothly thanks to the generosity of Chief M.K.O. Abiola, a Nigerian businessman and philanthropist, and the Oakdale Trust.

The social backgrounds of Hibiscus clients

In December 1992, Hibiscus had dealt with 48 cases, 39 of whom were women whose ages ranged between 29 and 57 years. Over

60 percent were below 40 years old. Only 6 were married, while 33 were single parents. Twenty-five had either divorced or separated from their husbands while 8 of them were widowed. Between them, these clients had 155 children whose ages ranged between 7 months and 26 years. Fifty three were under 8 years old while 71 were between 8 and 17 and 31 were over 17 years old. Sixteen of the children were in tertiary institutions; 49 in secondary grammar schools; 6 were in vocational trade classes; 56 in primary schools and 18 were under school age. Seven of the women were married, while 9 were unemployed. Since this date the Hibiscus workload has increased, with 30 new clients in 1993. However, the patterns remain as above.[2]

While it is difficult to determine precisely the incomes of women, anecdotal evidence suggests that their situations were far from comfortable. Of those employed (as teachers or professional traders), earning power had been seriously eroded by the economic crisis in Nigeria which involved massive currency devaluation and escalating inflation.[3] Some had lost jobs, while divorce and separation from husbands had made several into sole providers for their families. Of the few who were married, some had unemployed spouses. The pressure to find money for educating children has increased enormously following the introduction of school fees in 1986. To such women, the temptation to earn one thousand pounds (now almost one hundred and thirty thousand Naira) often proved irresistible.

These women, like millions of other poor, and even middle-class, Nigerians, are victims of an economic crisis which has seen per-capita income fall from over $US 1,000 per annum in 1980, to less than $300 in 1995 (see Joshua, this volume). In the same period inflation has risen from less than 10 percent to almost 100 percent, putting essential commodities out of reach for all but the small minority of very rich. The local currency, the Naira, which was worth almost $2 in 1980, is now worth about 4 cents officially and one cent in the black market and bureaux de change. Nigerians now have to pay fees for health and education, which were free in the period of the oil 'boom'. With the economy on the verge of collapse, with capacity utilization down to 30 percent or less, many Nigerians who would have pursued legitimate economic activities are now involved in fraud and the drug trade.[4]

But while the drug 'barons', who operate as big-businessmen

and women, are rarely caught, it is the Nigerian poor (or relatively poor) hired to carry relatively small quantities of drugs, who pay the penalty. In attempting to help their dependents and loved ones overcome abject poverty, these couriers may be imprisoned for years, exacerbating the very conditions they were seeking to alleviate.

Robbed of their mothers or providers for many years, the condition of the children and other dependents is tragic. Many children are forced to leave school, while others face starvation or homelessness. These hardships are often experienced without the social welfare cushion of the traditional extended family, and without a State system of welfare services to replace it.

The Lagos office of Hibiscus was established in May 1991 to help overcome some of these difficulties. Two social workers, I.O. Okulaja[5] and S. S. Akinlana, supported by a secretary and office attendant, help the organization fulfil its objectives and aspirations. They paid a total of 250 visits to the dependents of our clients between 1991 and 1993, to provide needed support and assistance.

Having established itself by winning the trust of the clients and their dependents, Hibiscus is now in a position to provide background information for Pre-Sentence Reports on arrested drug courier suspects for the British courts. The Home Office and the judiciary regularly consult FPWP and Hibiscus on the problems of women on trial or in prison, and there have been some visible improvements in the condition of these women, especially since the Criminal Justice Act 1991 came into force in October 1992. Several women have been given parole, while the background information used in the courts has helped towards reduced sentences as well as assisting general welfare by enabling a constant liaison between women in this country and their families at home.[6]

The broadcast of the BBC television documentary 'Mules' on 27 October 1992 also served to increase public awareness in the U.K. and abroad on the consequences and effects of drug trafficking. 'Mules', made by Olivia Lichtenstein for the BBC, was apparently videotaped by the Nigerian High Commission in London and shown on Nigerian television where it received a very lively response. After the broadcast, FPWP was overwhelmed by callers seeking more information and offering assistance. The documentary focused on the problems of Nigerian women who had been imprisoned for attempting to import drugs into the United Kingdom and the role of Hibiscus in trying to assist them. It covered the activities of the Hibiscus office and staff in Lagos, as well as interviewing Nigerian Government Officials involved in Social Welfare. Since its broadcast, the Judiciary seems to have become more sensitive to the cases of arrested or imprisoned women, and the public, particularly the Nigerian community in Britain, have become more aware of the problems faced by Nigerian women in custody and the consequences of drug importation.

Conclusion

So far Hibiscus has lived up to expectations in fulfilling the objectives for which it was established. So successful has it been that in January 1994 a branch was set up in Jamaica, which follows Nigeria in the numbers of their nationals incarcerated in British prisons. While the organization has not been able to achieve all that it envisaged, the relief it has been able to afford some of the women and their dependents is very satisfying indeed.

Hibiscus' constant support to foreign nationals in prison (especially Nigerians and Jamaicans), has enabled them to sustain relationships with their families and communities, making their lives more tolerable in prison and assisting their rehabilitation when they return home. This is achieved through ongoing support, by visiting their families giving advice on child care, helping them to come to terms with the unplanned separation of their breadwinner, and helping them to cope with existing problems brought on by their absence.

Hibiscus encourages constant visits and home leaves, and gives support to the families of prisoners who are experiencing difficulties, sometimes by doing something as simple as arranging a phone call. This helps both the prisoners and their families to come to terms with the trauma of confinement and separation.

However, serious problems remain. Funding has been difficult because of the reluctance of the Home Office and some charitable trusts to provide resources for the benefit of foreign women who are considered to have offended against the laws of the United Kingdom. Efforts will continue to convince these funding bodies and agencies that Hibiscus' work in educating the public in Britain and abroad on the effects of drug trafficking will help to reduce many of the problems associated with the trade.

As well as saving British tax-payers' money, it would be far more humane for these women to serve their sentences in their home country where they would be close to their relatives. But this is not possible at present because there is no repatriation agreement between the UK and Nigeria. Such an agreement is unlikely in the near future because Nigeria's decree 33 makes drug-trafficking a far more serious offence, for which the women could be re-imprisoned upon return to Nigeria, even after serving their sentences in Britain. The state of Nigerian prisons is also much worse than that of British prisons, and some women prefer not to be sent home where the misery and stigma of imprisonment would be so much greater.

Nigerian women, who constitute a large percentage of women in prison, face peculiar problems. Although English is the official language of their country, only a small minority speak it well. Interpreting facilities for over 250 Nigerian languages are limited or non-existent, resulting in serious disadvantage in courts and police stations, and serious isolation and discrimination in prison. Although Nigeria is a six-hour plane flight away, the poverty of relatives and friends mean that family and other visits are practically impossible. Residing in a tropical climate, the women who come on what they think will be very short visits have made no plans for the very harsh winters in an alien and inhospitable country. They lack money for clothes, and family and other support systems which are necessary to survive in a land they cannot call home.

But the most serious problem of all, which is entirely beyond the control of Hibiscus, is the poverty experienced by so many in countries like Nigeria, Jamaica and Colombia. This poverty contributes heavily to these women's decisions to resort to such desperate measures as drug smuggling. Until these conditions are alleviated, organisations like Hibiscus will soldier on, hoping for the best, while praying that things will not get worse.

Notes

1. See the Annual Report of FPWP and Hibiscus for 1992/93. It is possible that variations are due to a degree of cooperation with Customs and Excise, such as providing intelligence. Confessions and guilty pleas could result in reduced sentences.
2. FPWP (Hibiscus) Annual Report 1993/4.
3. See for example 'Nigeria to 2000: After The Generals' Economist Intelligence Unit, London 1995; 'Oil Stirs up Troubled Waters', Financial Times, London, 26 July 1995.
4. ibid.
5. Isaac Okulaja, the hard-working, mature and dedicated social worker who did so much to make the Lagos office of Hibiscus a success, died on 30 June 1995. May his soul rest in perfect peace.
6. The Home Office Minister, David MacLean, tabled an amendment in February 1994 to the Criminal Justice and Public Order Bill effectively removing the compulsion on courts to obtain pre-sentence reports (see Hammond, this volume). As a result, sentencing might revert to the mechanical elements of the quantity of drugs and co-operation with Customs and Excise Police, without consideration of extenuating circumstances such as lack of education, social background and vulnerability, especially of abused women.

III

Perspectives on Law Enforcement

1
Drug Markets and Law Enforcement in Europe

Nicholas Dorn

Introduction

What will be the effects of the Single Market of the European Communities as far as drug trafficking goes? Most commentators seem to suggest that the changes in Europe open the door to greater drug problems, including the growth of bigger drug trafficking organizations. I believe the opposite to be the case.

There are four main points in my argument. First, I suggest that consideration of the implications of the Single Market of the European Communities (EC), may be useful for understanding the options for drug markets and for drug enforcement. Second, I touch upon the debate about the consequences of the 1992 process upon drug trafficking in Europe, and suggest that these consequences may be more subtle than often supposed. Third, I turn to the implication of the Single Market for the future development of policing and drug enforcement in Europe. In conclusion, I suggest that these historic changes will reduce the chances of large criminal organisations coming to dominate drug traffic in the European Community and that the Single Market is good news for policing, and bad news for big trafficking organizations.

The double impact of the single market

So far, the historical project of European union has reached the stage of Economic Union, with the creation of a Common Market

170

or Single Market for goods, workers, services and capital. Whatever happens in relation to Maastricht, the completion of the Single Market will continue, as foreseen by the Treaty of Rome and the Single European Act. I start by asking: what will be the impact of the Single Market of the European Communities (EC), upon drug trafficking?

There are two sides to this question. First, there is the idea that the Single Market of the EC will stimulate a great increase in crimes, such as drug trafficking, across the continent of Europe. Indeed, there has been considerable public and political debate about the consequences of the free movement of goods and persons, as far as drug trafficking is concerned. Some observers even suggest we will face some kind of 'Euro-Mafia'. Second, as a response to the Single Market, EC Member States are cooperating in a reorganisation of the functioning and structures of policing in Europe. Since criminals can only stay in business if they adapt their activities to their environment, the successful criminal changes as policing changes. So, any changes in policing will bring about changes in crime.

The impact of free movement upon drug trafficking

Many people suggest that the single market will cause a quantitative increase in drug trafficking. This hypothesis fits in with the resurgence of nationalistic feelings in Europe and Eastern Europe, with the suspicion of all things 'foreign'. Also, it may be said to be functional for police agencies, since a European-wide wave of concern over free movement and trafficking may help to release financial resources for policing, and may legitimise the creation of new police powers.[1]

But just because the hypothesis is popular, that does not mean that it corresponds to reality. The movements of criminals will continue to be restricted by informal factors, such as culture, language and criminal opportunity. In order to operate successfully in a country, it is necessary to be familiar with its mores and culture, and to be competent in presenting oneself. Such competence is not easy to achieve, when moving from one's country and region of origin, to other parts of the EC. And, once one has become culturally competent in the new environment, it takes time to make criminal contacts, to gain trust, and to get used to local police and their tactics, and so on. In general, we can say that criminality does not travel well.

Also, many of the compensatory measures being discussed – first by the Schengen countries, then by the whole EC, measures precisely designed to compensate for the abolition of internal borders – will make it *more difficult* for criminals to move around Europe without leaving a trace of their activities. For example, identity cards, hotel registers, and financial records all restrict the ability of even sophisticated criminals to move about without leaving a trail which may be checked through police information systems. These control and cultural factors, can be expected to restrict the impact of 1993 upon the free movement of criminals.

Whatever happens to the quantitative level of crime as a result of free movement in Europe, we may reasonably expect to see some *qualitative* adjustments in the ways in which criminals organize and operate.[2]

From a criminological point of view, changes in the pattern of crime as a result of free movement might be:

- spatial changes (changes in the geographical distributions of crime);

- personnel changes (changes in the types of persons involved in various branches of crime); or

- crime type changes (changes in the sorts of crime that are committed, as a response to free movement).

(a) Spatial changes

Some spatial changes in the pattern of crime might occur, since free movement for EC citizens will mean the possibility of criminals moving from one area of the EC to another, with slightly greater ease than before. This may not mean more crime, but it could perhaps mean a **relocation** of criminal acts. However, as noted above, 'compensatory measures' are likely to generate more records on EC and other nationals, as they use hotels, financial services and other services. Compensatory measures *may induce them to stay at home*, more than they do today.

(b) Personnel changes

Curiously, it may be the least sophisticated criminals – those who have no legitimate business 'front' or respectable identity, and who must move through the *irregular economy* (grey, or underground economy) – who may be more able to move about without detection in the Single Market. We can link this possibility to the question of migrants moving between countries in search of legitimate work, but who may not always be successful in getting such work, and who may therefore come into contact with the irregular economy, and the possibilities for crime.

In the light of these considerations, I suggest that free movement may be linked to low-end criminality (for example, low level drug trafficking) – but not with higher-level crime (for example, higher level drug trafficking). This is the opposite of the usual idea of criminal syndicates moving around Europe, but it seems just as good as a hypothesis!

(c) Crime type changes

Several authorities have established that the removal (or lowering) of internal borders provides a stimulus to certain kinds of financial crime in the EC, particularly fraud related to Value Added Tax (VAT). This occurs because differences in the levels of VAT between two Member States provide an incentive to switch goods from the low-tax country, selling them in the higher-tax country, and profiting by the difference. It is regarded as impossible for the authorities to keep track of every consignment of goods, so checks can be made in only a small minority of cases. This means that tax frauds will necessarily continue, as long as we have open borders and different VAT rates.

What, then, about drug trafficking from one country to another? Will this not increase in the Single Market? The answer to this is probably 'No'. This is because the internal borders themselves yield relatively little intelligence about drug trafficking. The more significant seizures of drugs result from police or Customs intelligence that has been generated from other sources. In the past, seizures have generally been made at the borders for reasons of convenience, or to credit the operation clearly to Customs agencies. But, increasingly over the past decade, 'controlled deliveries' of drugs occur, where the consignment is allowed to proceed through the border under surveillance (see Albrecht, this volume).

This allows police and Customs to identify the people receiving the drugs – and perhaps even to apprehend the next customer along, and so on.

This may be called 'across market policing' and 'down market policing'.[3] It is potentially more productive than rigid border enforcement. Thus, we can say that the development of modern policing methods and cooperation has made the internal borders increasingly redundant as far as drug trafficking is concerned.[4] In these circumstances, we may conclude that 1992 is unlikely to stimulate inter-state drug trafficking within the EC.

Therefore, the abolition or lowering of internal borders in the EC, as part of the creation of a Single Market, will probably *not* cause any increase in the movements of 'Big Traffickers' around the EC, nor the amounts of drugs being smuggled from one EC country to another.

On the other hand, poorly qualified job-seekers, failing to find employment with wages high enough to meet their expenses in their new country, may become pushed down into the irregular economy – for example, into local, low-level drug dealing. Police attention to such activities, and mass media coverage, is likely to raise social tensions throughout the EC.

The single market and police co-operation

There are three main European arenas in which police cooperation is being encouraged: the TREVI group, the Schengen group and Maastricht.

i) TREVI
As EC countries move towards some degree of European Union – and as they pass through a sufficient stage of economic and social union to become a single market without internal frontiers – they develop different ideas about territoriality. Less and less do they regard each others' territory as wholly 'foreign', when police cooperation is a topic for inter-government negotiation between their foreign ministers. More and more, they regard such territory as at least partly 'domestic', and regard police cooperation as a matter for negotiation between Justice/Interior Ministries – even directly between police agencies themselves.

Thus, at the level of the whole EC, it was the foreign ministers, meeting in the context of the European Political Cooperation (EPC) in 1975, who first perceived a need for police cooperation. They then invited Interior Ministers to meet together with representatives of the police to constitute the TREVI group. This group is an important meeting place for EC police agencies and their Ministries. TREVI began with a focus on terrorism, and in 1985 it set up subgroups on international crime such as armed robberies and on drug trafficking. In 1986, the European Council of Foreign Ministers resolved to coordinate TREVI through the group of three Ministers who constitute the EC Troika (made up of the present president of the Council, together with the previous president, and the next in line).

In 1989, TREVI agreed cooperation on police training, technology, information exchange and liaison officers, which provided the framework within which the European Police Office, *Europol*, was to be established.

ii) Schengen
Whilst TREVI concerns itself primarily with policing matters, the Schengen Agreement (1985) and Convention (1990) covers a much wider swathe of criminal justice cooperation in Europe. As well as agreements on police powers to operate across internal EC borders, there are limited attempts at harmonization of some aspects of criminal law.

The origins of Schengen lie back in 1960, when Belgium, the Netherlands and Luxembourg abolished their common borders, transferring controls to their common *external* frontiers, and to various internal spot-checks. They were joined from 1980 by France and Germany, and the five countries signed the Schengen Agreement. The Secretariat of the Benelux Economic Union facilitated negotiations within four working groups concerned with police and security matters, movement of persons, transport, and movement of goods. In 1990, the parties signed the Schengen Convention, implementing the 1985 Agreement, subject to Parliamentary agreement in each country.

The Schengen Convention regulates the exchange of information; permits undercover officers to continue their surveillance across borders; and allows 'hot pursuit' of criminals across borders. Additionally, the prosecuting authorities of Schengen countries may communicate requests directly, rather than through their Foreign Ministries. And there is a degree of harmonization of conditions for mutual assistance in search and seizure of evidence. These are all *procedural* aspects of criminal justice; the extent of harmonisation of legislation on substantive aspects of criminal law is minimal.[5] Additionally, the countries involved set up the Schengen Information System (SIS), which acts as a channel for the exchange of police and immigration information on Persons Wanted, and requests for information and assistance.[6] With the accession of Spain, Portugal and Italy to Schengen, the SIS forms the basis for a European Information System (the EIS).[7]

iii) Maastricht
The Maastricht Treaty contains several quite separate sections:[8]

- Title II covers amendments to the Treaty of Rome, concerning various trade matters and Monetary Union;

- Title V is entitled 'Provisions on a Common Foreign and Security Policy'; and

- Title VI covers 'Provisions on Cooperation in the Spheres of Justice and Home Affairs'.

Title II of the Treaty explicitly *excludes* 'any harmonization of the laws or regulation of Member States' on health or treatment aspects of European drug policy. It merely speaks of *cooperation* on health protection and prevention issues, anticipating European-wide publicity campaigns, such as European Drug Prevention Week. This is no more than synchronized flag-waving. Beneath the flags, the health and welfare policies of member states in relation to drug users may, or may not, converge, as each Member State decides. The principle of subsidiarity applies here. So the Dutch can go on with their health policy ('tolerance'); the Norwegians can go with theirs (similar to the American policy of 'zero tolerance'); and in Italy you can also do whatever pleases you – as far as health policy towards drug users is concerned.

But, in relation to crime, especially serious crime such as drug trafficking, all member states are going down the same route. Title VI, setting out *Provisions on Cooperation in the Spheres of Justice and Home Affairs*, is very favourable to closer cooperation and convergence in the European Community. Reflecting the trend established by the Schengen countries and by International Conventions, Maastricht foresees greater police cooperation and judicial cooperation. The Treaty does *not* rule out actual harmonization of criminal law and civil law within Europe, and foresees a potential role for the European Court of Justice, in the interpretation of European and other Conventions on crime control.[9]

Thus, we can see that criminal justice policy – and particularly police action against drug traffickers – is the historical site for the convergence and eventual harmonization of EC drug policy. Health policy on drug users may be locally determined, but all Member States are going down the one road, as far as policing and anti-trafficking actions are concerned.

It seems fairly clear that, even if political turbulence in various countries of the EC should result in the Treaty not being ratified as far as Title II on Economic and Monetary Union is concerned, the cooperation on Justice and Home Affairs, as set out in Title VI, *will go ahead*. This part of the Treaty declares that:

> For the purpose of achieving the objectives of the Union, in particular the free movement of persons, and without prejudice to the powers of the European Community, Member States shall regard the following areas as matters of common interest ... 1) asylum policy ... 2) the external borders ... 3) immigration policy ... 4) drug addiction (excluding police cooperation on trafficking) 5) fraud (excluding police cooperation) ... 6) judicial cooperation in civil matters ... 7) judicial cooperation in criminal matters, 8) Customs cooperation, and 9) aspects of police cooperation. (treaty on European Union, 1991, Title VI, Article K.1, paras 1–6, parts of)

In these matters, the Council may promote any cooperation, adopt any joint action, and draft Conventions which it shall recommend to Member States to adopt, by a two-thirds majority of Council (Article K.3).[10]

As far as police cooperation is concerned, Member States foresee:

> Police cooperation for the purposes of preventing and combatting terrorism, unlawful drug trafficking and other serious forms of international crime including, if necessary, certain aspects of

Customs cooperation in connection with the organisation of a Union-wide system for exchanging information within a European Police Office ... (Article K.1 para 9)

This is Europol, as envisaged by the TREVI group. Europol's first priority will be to act as a secure channel for the exchange of *intelligence* in relation to drug trafficking into, and within, EC countries.[11] Finally, Title VI does not rule out the possibility of harmonization of the criminal and civil laws of Member States.

Linkage, convergence and harmonization: framework for EC policing

Within the TREVI group and the Schengen and Maastricht agreements, we see the framework of policing in Europe:

i) A quite public regulatory framework for cooperation of police and prosecution agencies as they cooperate across EC internal borders, and exchange routine information (Schengen Agreement and Convention);

ii) A very private framework for police exchange of training, methodologies of investigation, intelligence gathering and analysis, and future strategies (TREVI, leading to Europol); and

iii) Agreement in principle on the possibility of a pan-European system of Criminal Justice, with harmonization of civil and criminal legislation, and a role for the European Court of Justice (Maastricht, developing both Schengen and TREVI).

In other words, the police services and criminal justice systems of EC countries are becoming:

- increasingly *linked through information systems*;

- rapidly *converging* in their methodologies;

- and, more slowly, becoming *harmonized* in terms of their formal rules.

That is to say, more and more, the various policing services of EC Member States are able to operate in each other's 'legal space', right across the EC. Instead of the main police service of each Member State having a monopoly of policing in its own country, the policing services of the EC are beginning to *share* the task of law enforcement throughout the EC.

However, the policing systems of the Member States are remaining *independent* of each other. It seems unlikely that European police and Customs services would actually merge into one big organization. Instead, by overlooking each other's territories and actions, police services in Europe are developing 'multiple jurisdiction'.[12] This has significant consequences for the future pattern of crimes, such as drug trafficking, in Europe.

The consequences of multiple jurisdiction

Criminologists have studied the effect that police organization has on criminality. Generally speaking, the literature suggests that large criminal organizations, criminal monopolies, 'cartels', and so on, can only persist where there is one major, monopoly, law enforcement organization. This is because a single law enforcement agency can be 'bought off', when key individuals in it are bribed, or otherwise quietened. As my colleagues and I have put it:

> In both the United States and Britain, there has been a movement away from sole jurisdiction (one agency) in law enforcement towards *multiple jurisdiction*, which means that several different agencies share responsibility for policing of any given geographical area. The trend is partly a response to the problem of corruption: if there is just one agency to 'buy off', then corruption is relatively easy – as illustrated by the wave of scandals in the New York Police Department leading to the Knapp Commission, and by the (relatively minor) scandals in the Metropolitan Police Drug Squad in London in the 1970s.[13]

On the other hand, if there are a variety of law enforcement agencies, alongside each other, each looking at each other as well as at the criminals, then the prospects for corruption are much reduced. No criminal monopoly can emerge. This is because 'no single (police) agency can issue a licence for an illegal operator'.[14]

Similarly, in Britain, my colleagues and I have argued in the following terms:

> Today in Britain, for example, medium scale drug dealing may attract a local drug squad, an area drug squad, a regional squad, a liaison officer from the National Drugs Intelligence Unit, and possibly Customs and Excise. In such conditions, with several agencies 'fishing in the same pool', any one agency that is corrupted into protecting a drug distribution enterprise will sooner or later quite likely have such corruption discovered by one of the other agencies. The result is that *major* corruption of the kind needed to protect a large or monopolistic (criminal) enterprise cannot easily be carried out.[15]

Transferring this to the context of crime control in the European Community, one can think along the following lines: any over-centralization of police services at European level might lead to a monopoly of policing services, corruption of this Euro-police force, and the emergence of a large, trans-European, Mafia-like, criminal organization; but, with many different police agencies involved in the control of trafficking and other major crimes in Europe, there will be no monopoly police agency, and so much less opportunity for corruption. There will be no Euro-Mafia.

Conclusion

This article has two broad conclusions:

1) The Single Market of 1993 may cause an increase in low level crime, such as local, retail selling of drugs – but not the explosion of higher level crime, such as major drug trafficking, that has sometimes been predicted. In this sense, the consequences of 1993 may be more mundane, and less spectacular, than expected.

2) On the policing side, the Single Market provides a framework for increasing linkage, convergence and harmonisation – lead-

ing to some degree of multiple jurisdiction between policing services across the EC. Such a development will cut down the dangers of corruption that accompany monopoly crime control agencies.

These two possibilities together imply that, in spite of the fact that the drug problem in Europe may look bad today, it will *not* get much worse in future – at least as far as major trafficking is concerned.

It is therefore no longer necessary to speak of a War, or to adopt any measure that is not carefully considered. In this part of history, we have some time to think. We can ask – where shall we go from here?

Notes

1. Some observers claim that since police and prosecutors' powers and their cooperation in Europe are increasing, whilst the rights of defendants and the powers of defence solicitors stand still, the balance is shifting too far against the defence. Whether this is true or not, it can be clearly seen that a debate about the Single Market encouraging crime is to the advantage of policing agencies generally, in their battle for powers and resources.
2. As one recent Conference agreed, 'no consequent *upsurge* in criminal activity should be anticipated, [but] the changes associated with 1992 could lead to changes in the *pattern* of criminal behaviour' (Latter, R., 1990, *Crime and the European Community after 1992*, Wilton Park papers 31, London: HMSO; 2).
3. Dorn, Murji and South, *Traffickers*, Routledge, 1991.
4. The tactic of 'letting the drugs run', making a controlled delivery, and maximising the number of subsequent arrests, can only be adopted when police and Customs both sides of a border have good drugs intelligence, and can cooperate well. So, where political conditions or undeveloped policing agencies in a 'source country' make it difficult to generate reliable intelligence or to maintain secrecy of a police operation, border checks remain necessary. An example of this is given by the recent history of trafficking from Panama to the United States, where efforts at police cooperation appear to have undermined US high level political support for General Noriega.
5. On drugs legislation, Schengen is quite unremarkable. It re-affirms each country's existing commitment to fight against large-scale or international trafficking – and it obliges each country to take care to do nothing that might encourage the illicit import or export of drugs between the countries. But the social features of each country's policies on demand-reduction, control of the retail-level trade, and treatment policies are respected by Schengen.
6. The main differences between the SIS/EIS and Europol are: the SIS/EIS carries *information* about a variety of notices such as Persons Wanted; but Europol is a more restricted *intelligence* network, covering suspected criminals and

their associates who are potential targets for investigation, intelligence reports, and so on.

7. The Danish referendum 'No' to Maastricht throws into doubt the full implementation of Schengen which, like Maastricht, must be ratified through Parliamentary approval. The debate in the Netherlands and the Nordic countries has already been quite vigorous. Whatever happens on Schengen and on the economic and monetary Title of Maastricht, the amendments to the Treaty of Rome already agreed by the Single European Act have a momentum of their own. As one author has observed, 'the achievements of Schengen would eventually have to yield to legal arrangements applicable to all EC Member States' (Schutte, J., 1991, 'Schengen: its meaning for the free movement of persons in Europe', *Common Market Law Review*, 28; 549–570.) To cut a long story short, even if Schengen falls by the wayside, its provisions will be carried forward by other inter-governmental agreements and by EC Directives and Regulations. In this sense, Schengen, like TREVI, is the shape of the future.

8. And an Annex, covering a number of Protocols (including one on Social Policy signed by eleven out of the twelve EC Member States).

9. Such interpretation is allowed for by Article 177 of the Treaty of Rome. However, no enforcement mechanism is given by this Article of the Treaty, so the European Court of Justice (ECJ) would be able to bring only moral pressure against member states which failed to implement Conventions correctly. The ECJ has fuller powers only on those matters which are covered by the development of competence on trade and social matters, such as money laundering or and precursor chemical control.

10. Notably, it is acknowledged that the Commission may propose Community legislation such as Directives and Regulations and, correspondingly, achieve harmonization of domestic legislation, on such Home Affairs matters as 'drug addiction' (that is to say, control of drug *users*, but not police cooperation against *traffickers* – see below).

11. As far as the Justice and Home Affairs part of Maastricht goes, the European Court of Justice is recognized as having a *potential* role in interpretation of any conflicts or uncertainty regarding Community legislation on Justice and Home Affairs – including criminal law, and policing. 'Such Conventions (as the Council may recommend to Member States on civil or criminal law matters, or police cooperation) may stipulate that the Court of Justice shall have jurisdiction to interpret their provisions and to rule on any disputes regarding their application . . .' (Article K.3, Paragraph 2c). The Court of Justice would then have to take into account certain safeguards provided for in other Conventions to which the Member States are signatories. Article K.2 (1) states that 'The matters referred to . . . shall be dealt with in compliance with the European Convention for the Protection of Human Rights and Fundamental Freedoms of 4 November 1950 and the Convention relating to the Status of Refugees of 28 July 1951 and having regard to the protection afforded by Member States to persons persecuted on political grounds'. Such compliance should not prove difficult for the Court. The constraint of acting in compliance with the Human Rights Convention has already been taken on to some extent by the EC Court through its development of EC jurisprudence (particularly in a series of references from the German Constitutional Court).

12. Punch, M., 1985, *Conduct Unbecoming; the social construction of police deviance*, London: Tavistock.

182

13. Dorn, N., and South, N., 1990, 'Drug markets and law enforcement', *British Journal of Criminology*, 30, 2, Spring; 171–188.
14. Reuter, R., 1983, *Disorganised Crime: illegal markets and the Mafia*, Mass: MIT Press.
15. Dorn and South, *op. cit.*

2
Drug Couriers and the Role of Customs and Excise:
A Customs Senior Manager's Personal View

Dennis A. Walton[1]

Introduction

Customs is a very old Department with written records of our activity going back to the 8th century. Although written records only go back that far there is overwhelming evidence of an even longer history dating back to Biblical times and before. Indeed it has been suggested that Customs, with its tax collecting history, is probably the second oldest profession of all. Excise on the other hand is relatively new, an import from Holland, introduced by Oliver Cromwell to finance his army.

Of course it is in respect of collection of revenue that Customs and Excise are probably best known and that is why the words 'Have you anything to declare?' are indelibly inscribed on the memories of so many, otherwise law-abiding citizens, who have succumbed to the temptation to smuggle relatively minor items and been surprised at the severity of penalties when caught.

Over the centuries Customs and Excise have collected a bewildering array of other responsibilities with little or nothing to do with revenue collection simply because they were there at the frontiers with powers enabling us to examine all or any of the goods or people entering our country. It made sense and proved an economical and effective way to enforce a wide variety of laws and regulations.

During the last few decades these additional responsibilities have included more and more activities which may be loosely described as designed to 'protect society'. Restrictions policed at the frontiers have been designed to protect society from the import of such things as obscene material, diseased plants or animal products, offensive weapons, explosives, rabid animals, artefacts from the endangered species and a whole host of other, undesirable imports. Chief amongst these over the last two decades has been controlled drugs.

The scourge of illicit drug-trafficking has become such a threat, such a matter for national and international concern that now, in the Customs management plan, the old and the new rank alongside each other as our first priorities for action: ie. collecting of the major revenues and countering trafficking in illicit drugs. This is fully in line with the Government's Strategy as set out in the 1995 White Paper 'Tackling Drugs Together'. Our role within the strategy consists of:

1. preventing and detecting the illegal import and export of controlled drugs;

2. investigating and prosecuting organizations and individuals engaged in drug smuggling;

3. identifying the proceeds of such crime.

The role of Customs and Excise in countering drug trafficking

As with other prohibitions and restrictions, one of our principal aims is to prevent the importation of goods which are prohibited. In the days when we stopped and confronted every passenger and examined every vehicle, vessel or aircraft entering or leaving our territory, I suppose this was a reasonable aim. But of course, even in those days 100 percent success could not be guaranteed and some prohibited goods including drugs would get through. The last 2 or 3 decades have seen such an explosive growth of international traffic of all sorts that this confrontational control of imports and exports had to go. No longer could we take the time to look at everyone and everything entering or leaving the UK. International movement of goods in particular is the lifeblood of many countries' economies and new, selective controls had to be applied.

Obviously this opened the door much wider to illegal imports and this development coincided with the growth of drug trafficking at an alarming and socially destructive rate. Customs could no longer even pretend that they could keep the lid on illegal importation of drugs by the simple aim of prevention. Our aims, objectives and methods had to change and they have done.

Our checks at frontiers no longer depend upon an individual assessment of each and every person or consignment crossing our borders. Rather we depend upon information, often through computers, intelligence, selective application of controls, and cooperation with other enforcement agencies at home – notably the police – and abroad. The success of our lead in this field is evident in the record seizures of illicit drugs in recent years and in our continually growing involvement in joint operations with the police at home and in joint operations with other enforcement agencies abroad. But, of course, there is no room for complacency.

Customs objectives today

Our objectives in countering drug trafficking today are much more far reaching and all-embracing. Of course, we must still try to prevent as much as possible from entering the UK. But that is only a start. Our objectives go on from there to:

1. prevent illicit drugs from entering the UK;

2. apprehend and prosecute those attempting to smuggle drugs;

3. assist, where appropriate, the police to investigate;

4. with international cooperation, investigate the supply lines;

5. identify and prosecute those in *organisations* responsible for trafficking;

6. trace, freeze and seize assets of traffickers; and

186

7. establish and enhance inter-agency and international information exchange systems.

You will see from this that the drug courier, although often a
'bit part' player in the scenario, may have a vital role in the
commencement of effective enforcement action.

Couriers

It is wrong to think of 'Couriers' always as simple 'Mules' who
carry the goods for others. Of course some of them are just that:
people who have been tempted, hired, coerced or even compelled
by threat, intimidation, violence or whatever to do what others
demand. But some are integral parts of the network. Rarely are
they prime movers in the scheme. Customs work includes trying
to assess just what their role is in the larger scene. The smugglers
will rarely admit if they have a larger role than is apparent and,
in common with smugglers down the ages, of whatever goods,
will often fall back on one of three classic excuses: 'I didn't know
it was illegal', 'I didn't know what I was carrying' or 'Someone
else packed the goods'.

Naturally linguistic difficulties can make for problems in our
assessment of a courier's role, but I should emphasize the importance we place upon the availability of interpreters and our good
fortune in having officers from a wide range of ethnic origins who
bring with them vital linguistic skills for the interrogation of
people whose command of English is poor. As a cynic with more
than 36 years' service in Customs behind me may I just comment
how dramatically some suspected smugglers' comprehension of
English improves when they are confronted by an officer who
speaks their language fluently.

Nevertheless, there are severe problems with the 'genuine' couriers who really know little or nothing about the organization they
serve. Their knowledge of the supply side may be limited to the
equivalent of 'I got the package(s) from a guy I know as Tom Smith
in a pub somewhere down the Old Kent Road' or 'from Hans
Schmidt in a bar in Amsterdam'. Their knowledge of what will
happen in the UK after their arrival may be even less in that they
are simply told to go to an address and wait to be contacted. Where

we can, of course, we follow up any leads at home or abroad in line with our objectives to identify the people behind the organizations. But, where the information about supply is not usable or where the interception of a courier must be obvious because of the 6, 7 or 8 days' wait while internally concealed drugs are expelled, there is little we can do to extend our investigation.

Customs treatment of couriers

Our treatment of drug couriers follows our pattern of treatment of any alleged smuggler with the only major difference being the special procedures necessary to deal with internal concealments. But even these conform to the requirements of the Police and Criminal Evidence Act 1984. Our aim is always to deal with anyone courteously, efficiently and professionally in the pursuance of our job, which is to ascertain the facts, reach a decision on whether or not an offence has been committed and, where appropriate, to prosecute the alleged offence through the Courts conforming to the precise requirements of the judicial system. It is not our job either to put forward or to suppress anything in mitigation except where a courier may voluntarily have provided information which proved to be helpful to further investigation. Such assistance will always be reported to the Court before sentencing. Any attempted interference with the judicial system over and beyond that would undoubtedly land us in very hot water indeed.

Of course, we have the opportunity at a policy level to discuss with other departments, principally the Home Office and, through them, the police, the changing aspects of drug trafficking and the need to modify our actions to meet current developments. At an operational level, this will be manifested through regular liaison, sharing of intelligence and planning of joint operations.

A response to Penny Green

I read Dr Green's report[2] with great interest and considerable sympathy for some of the opinions expressed and conclusions drawn. However, starting with the conclusions, I have to say that I think Dr Green has reached a conclusion about the drug trafficker which is as much an unjustified stereotype as that which she claims to be 'promulgated' – 'The ideological fusion of the courier with the wealthy drug profiteer . . .'. Make no mistake, a fair number of couriers are every bit as guilty as those running the organization behind them. They are full, participating partners in what I am sure most people recognize as an evil and degrading traffic.

At the other end of the scale of course there are weak, uneducated, underprivileged victims of criminal organizations. I am sure that I and others in our Department feel sympathy for them. But, as officials, our job is, as I have stated, to prosecute on the basis of facts and it must be right that we do so objectively leaving value judgement to those whose job it is – the Courts.

I read the section of Dr Green's report on Customs and Excise[3] with a certain wry amusement. I have already accused myself of cynicism and perhaps that is surfacing again. I have heard most of the excuses, accusations and mitigation many times before in many circumstances. In some cases in a previous incarnation, I have been responsible for evaluating the investigation of accusations of this nature [racism by Customs officers] – and let me assure you they are investigated rigorously. It would be very interesting if we could know the officer's account of the reported statements but, of course, without precise details of names and dates etc. we are not in a position to find out.

I am not saying that officers will not sometimes make injudicious remarks provoked by the unsavoury nature of the business they are dealing with. There is nothing pleasant about having to deal with drug couriers who have resorted to internal concealment. Officers are human and, in spite of rigorous training and close supervision in the field, they may occasionally over react. They would not be human otherwise. But I have every reason to believe that they carry out their duties in a very professional manner.

I must also take issue with two paragraphs in this section of the report. The third paragraph in the section reads as though there is an automatic and inexorable progression from stop to body search to urine test to X-ray followed by a '2–8 days wait'. That is far from the truth. The procedures will only be followed to that extent with either full consent of the passenger, Court approval, Court order or both. Similarly in the last paragraph on page 25 of the report it states 'She says she was interrogated without break from 3 pm until 1 am'. That may be her recollection of a traumatic experience but it is, quite simply, not possible. The rules governing custody, our instructions on supervision of those in custody, our interview procedures and everything else to do with custody are such that a 10 hour interrogation without a break is simply beyond belief. Apart from anything else, I do not believe any of our staff, no matter how they appear to the jaundiced eye of a detected smuggler, could be so inhumane.

I cannot let Section 6 of the report go unchallenged. I refer to the part entitled 'Seizures by Customs and Excise' on page 16. I regret that because we did not provide Dr Green with full information, she has reached dubious conclusions about our targeting policy. She rightly comments on the fact that 'The vast majority of Class A drug seizures are made from individual passengers'. In numerical terms that is undeniable. But if you examine closely the quantities seized over recent years you will see that the largest proportion of the weight of drugs seized comes from a smaller but still significant number of what we might call 'commercial seizures'. These are often the result of carefully planned intelligence-based operations. Both types of seizures are important and will continue to be within our policy. But I am afraid that I am still not going to disclose just what our policy is – for obvious reasons.

Equally I must comment on conclusions drawn in the same section on page 19 about confiscation orders. In using 1987 figures Dr Green has looked at the effects of the then new legislation, The Drug Trafficking Offences Act, 1986, rather soon after it came into force. I do not believe her conclusions stand the test of time. In 1992 there were about £41 million identified as benefits of drug trafficking, £29 million of suspected drug trafficking assets under restraint pending investigation and Customs total of confiscation orders to that date amounted to some £19 million. Of course traffickers do their best to conceal and protect their assets but both nationally and internationally groups, notably the Financial Action Task Force set up by G7 in 1989, are working to improve and strengthen legislation on this subject to counter the traffickers' efforts to preserve their assets.

Conclusion

I hope that in commenting on some of the implications of Dr Green's eminently readable and undoubtedly useful report I have not appeared unduly defensive. I do not intend to be nor do I see the need to be defensive. My intention was to set Customs actions in their proper context and to show the division which does and must lie between our function and those of others. It is not simply a case of 'following orders' blindly nor of 'it's more than my job's worth'. We have an important job to do in countering the evil trade of drug trafficking. We must always act within the law but humanely and courteously. We must not be tempted into trying to interfere with other aspects of procedures nor must we let them interfere with ours. It is at times a difficult balance but one which I believe we get right the vast majority of the time.

Notes

1. Denis Walton, now retired, is a former member of the Customs Directorate.
2. Penny Green, *Drug Couriers*, Howard League for Penal Reform, July 1991.
3. ibid., p. 25.

3
The Policing of Drugs in London:
A Police Commander's Personal View

John O'Connor[1]

Introduction

There are few subjects in the criminal code that have attracted as much research and debate as the misuse of dangerous drugs. Opinions abound from all quarters, including the law enforcement agencies, on the best way to deal with the problem. Similar debate has been going on in North America where the strategy of the 1970s and 1980s, appeared to be to attack the source. Government inspired programmes of crop destruction and encouragement of alternative crops have had little impact on the tide of drugs, especially cocaine, now saturating the American market. The Drug Enforcement Agency has now realised that the best way to tackle the problem is through demand reduction, and the only way to achieve that is through a coordinated strategy involving all of the agencies with an involvement, including education, health and local government.

The situation in London

So what is the situation today in London? Over 70 percent of all prosecutions and drug seizures occur within the boundaries of the Metropolitan Police, and my observations are focused on that force. Two main law enforcement agencies operate in the field of dangerous drugs, the Police and HM Customs and Excise. It has not been a happy marriage, more like living in sin, with no binding contract, and frequent rows and reconciliations. The drugs department of the Home Office, known as C5, tried to act as counsellor and honest broker, by producing a drug strategy which gave primacy to all importations and therefore primacy to HM Customs. The Police were unwilling to accept this, claiming that Customs were only interested in seizures and not dealer networks. Hopefully the development of the National Crime Intelligence System will resolve these differences. There are significant contributions to be made by both agencies in terms of manpower and resources, and it is in the interests of all parties to make sure it succeeds.

Surprisingly, the Metropolitan Police have no written strategy for dealing with the criminal misuse of drugs. They do, of course, have tactics and they have been successful in seizing large amounts of cocaine and heroin. They have also made significant inroads in combating amphetamine production, by establishing intelligence links with manufacturers and wholesalers of precursor chemicals which are used to produce amphetamine. Both Police and Customs have been successful in combating organized importations, and manufacture, of illegal substances. However, the impression given in some inner city areas is that drug dealing is rife, and the Police are doing little about it. It could legitimately be asked why the successes at the importation end are not being reflected by a reduction in supply to street dealers.

Diane Abbott, MP for Hackney, said during her talk on the politics of the war on drugs to the Howard League conference on drug couriers, that Police in her constituency appeared to operate a passive policy of containment which enabled a drugs culture to flourish, and could quickly go out of control. She likened Hackney and Stoke Newington to the drugs scene in Washington some years ago when a tactic of containment and appeasement led to a proliferation of drug abuse with disastrous consequences for the community. The advent of crack undoubtedly fuelled the problems in Washington.

The starting point of any research into criminal activity is to assess the size and scope of the problem. Before a meaningful strategy can be implemented the Police need to know precisely what it is they have to contend with. Professor David Grahame-Smith has been Chairman of the Advisory Council on the Misuse

of Drugs, (ACMD) since 1988. At a recent Association of Chief
Police Officers conference on drugs he stated that we do not have
accurate information on the scale of the problem or the number
of drug addicts. Intelligent guesses can be made within extremely
wide parameters, but it is a very inexact science.

It is reasonable to assume that if we do not know the size of
the problem, and we have little control over the market, then the
criminal misuse of drugs is virtually out of control. Responsibility
for this state of affairs lies collectively with the various agencies
involved in this field, and a breakdown in behavioural patterns of
many young people who feel they no longer have a stake in society.
It is not my intention to discuss the moral and sociological issues
which have been raised, but it is worth looking briefly at the
recent history of drugs law enforcement from a Metropolitan
Police perspective.

The development of drugs law enforcement

Misuse of drugs did not become a matter of major concern until
the late 1950s, and early 1960s. Cannabis was being widely used
by people in the pop music business. Young people using clubs
and discos wishing to stay awake all night became a ready market
for the pushers of amphetamines. Purple hearts, bombers and
dexadrines became part of the youth/drug culture. In the West End
of London arrests of youngsters for possessing these substances
was fairly easy because there were so many of them. Police officers
were able to make high numbers of arrests. These offences were
obviously not crimes against property, and did nothing to improve
the detection rate for burglaries and robberies. There was also
a growing tide of opinion led by some academics and medical
practitioners that cannabis was not harmful and should be
decriminalized. This pressure group climaxed with a full page
advertisement in The Times where many well-known personalities called for the legalization of cannabis. In the light of this
local Police chiefs became less interested in drugs and actively
discouraged officers from specifically targeting suspected drug
users.

At Scotland Yard a Central Drug Squad had been established for
some years. Some far-sighted members of that squad recognized

the emergence of disturbing trends. Top criminals were moving away from armed robbery and theft of high value loads, and were involved in financing importations of large amounts of drugs. The higher echelon of policy-makers did not respond quickly enough, and the Central Drug Squad remained under-resourced. Money was available to pay informants for crimes against property, but only a small amount was channelled to pay drugs informants. Technical support was not made freely available because drugs were not seen as a high priority demand. In fairness Police activities were directed at organized crime, and in particular armed robbery.

Some detectives resorted to paying informants with the seized drugs, or in some cases, with cash out of their own pockets. They tended to be informant led, and quite often the informants themselves were drug dealers wishing to remove the opposition. At this stage relations between HM Customs and Police were virtually non-existent, and the informant of one agency could well be the target of another. With this explosive cocktail of misconduct and mistrust Police and Customs were on a major collision course. This regrettable chapter in our history has been well reported and criminal prosecutions against police officers followed. Out of all this came proper informant handling guidelines, appropriate resourcing levels and an acknowledgement of the potential scale of the problem. Better international links with other agencies coordinated by the International Criminal Police Organization (Interpol) were established, and as a matter of priority improved co-operation between Police and Customs was seen as essential.

Developing a written strategy

At the time of writing (1992), the Metropolitan Police do not have a stated strategy. Assistant Commissioner Territorial Operations has commissioned a working party under my Chairmanship to produce such a document. What are we seeking to achieve? Under the general mandate of 'Making London Safer' we will produce a strategy which encompasses a realistic response to drug misuse, from solvent abuse by children to the organised criminals who arrange the importation and distribution of drugs. We need to reshape the market in order that we can exercise more control over it. A bottom-up approach will be recommended which will ensure the involvement of police at all levels. Crime prevention officers, and those involved in youth and community work, will liaise directly with the education authorities for an approved input at school on the dangers of solvent abuse. Sector policing will enable closer liaison with shopkeepers to take place, and information on the sale or theft of solvents will quickly be brought to our attention. We may be the first to know of a solvent abuse problem in a particular area, and initiate a joint strategy to deal with it.

We are looking at developing our partnership with local health authorities, and giving a priority to the health and well-being of drug dependents. The notion of treating addicts as victims may seem radical but young people who are offered and take drugs are very much the victims of the suppliers. Referral schemes and cautioning are the contribution we can make to the policy of ensuring that addicts keep free of disease, and do not become infected with HIV. There is a clear link between drug abuse and prostitution, and we need to ensure that drug abusers do not become the link for HIV to the community at large.

The supervised supply of pharmaceutically pure drugs in dependency clinics would have the effect of reducing the demand for drugs bought off the street. At the same time we will attack the street dealers by training selected officers in low level 'buy bust' techniques. It is intended to destabilize the security of the dealers by making them unsure as to whether they are dealing with a customer or an undercover police officer.

The arrival of crack cocaine has been a worrying development. It is a highly addictive derivative of cocaine which can be simply produced. Although the total amount of seizures have been relatively small the widespread use across many inner city areas is causing concern. It cannot be described as reaching epidemic proportions, but we must be prepared for an escalation in its use. The Metropolitan Police have established a Force Crack Intelligence Unit (now disbanded – Ed.) and it is intended that Area Drug Squads will be the operational arm.

Finally, at the upper level we shall be recommending that HM Customs and Excise and the Police set up joint task forces under the guidance of the National Crime Intelligence Service to ensure there is no conflict of interest.

Future prospects

For the future we should consider a more active demand reduction programme. Athletes are routinely tested for the presence of unlawful substances which enhance performance. In Chicago, police officers are routinely tested for the presence of drugs and a positive test means instant dismissal. Currently about 1 percent test positively. US Public Service employees are also subjected to the same procedures. Although the legality of such methods has been tested in the courts, the authorities have been upheld. These tactics are designed to frighten people away from drugs abuse and form a major plank in the strategy of demand reduction. In a recession with high unemployment, the fear of losing your job is a persuasive argument for not using drugs. One of the side effects of this programme in the US has been to polarize the community and thereby emphasize drug abuse in the ghettos. There is no discouragement to those who have no stake in society. The gap between the poor and the rest becomes greater. When the factor of race is added to the equation a hostile divide becomes positively dangerous.

Clearly such draconian methods are unlikely to be well received in London. We are not facing the scale of problem which exists in major US cities. But it is important that successful demand reduction programmes elsewhere do not result in making the United Kingdom an attractive alternative market. We do not have to follow US initiatives to the letter. For instance the introduction of Drugs Abuse Restriction Education (DARE) programme in Los Angeles and Chicago targets schools and warns of the dangers of drug abuse. In principle this sounds a good idea, but drug abuse by children of school age in Britain is not the same problem as in America. A scaled-down version of DARE approved by the education authorities would seem more appropriate to our needs.

Conclusion

Police and Customs are primarily concerned with illegal substances. However it is important that we are aware through research of other drug-related problems. Evidence has recently emerged which points to a possible link between steroid abuse and serious sexual assaults. Preliminary research has been conducted by Detective Inspector Bristow of the Metropolitan Police and her conclusions do give some cause for concern. The police may indeed be the first agency to recognize problems like this and they have a clear responsibility to advise the Home Office with a view to introducing new legislation.

Whatever strategies and tactics we adopt we have to be responsive to the needs of the whole community. The notion of treating addicts as victims will not be acceptable to the community at large if addicts are suspected of committing criminal offences to fund their habit. An apparently liberal approach by police may give the impression that we are condoning drug dependency clinics as havens for drug dealers. That perception is heightened when used needles and syringes are carelessly discarded in the vicinity of these centres. Before such a scheme can work we need to ensure close supervision and the goodwill of all the agencies involved.

Those working in the field of drug dependency are well aware of the difficulties of persuading people away from their habit. This is often a fruitless and frustrating exercise as many addicts will only move away from drugs when they have the desire to give up themselves. A sub-culture exists around social groups of drug dependents who are often jointly involved in crime and share the daily struggle for survival. There is often no acceptable alternative to their lifestyle and reform is unattractive. Beginning at the bottom with no skills and poor pay does not offer such encouragement to the addict who is willing to reform. Police activity must interlock with the strategies of other agencies if we are collectively going to be effective. Central government will have the lead role in urban regeneration programmes.

My sad conclusion is that drugs and their attendant problems will always be with us. I am not optimistic about the future. We, the police, realize that we need to improve our image and credibility with all sections of the community and it is recognized that we are in danger of becoming a despised service in the eyes of some people. We have made great strides to improve our quality of service in particular in the field of drugs law enforcement. There is much work still to be done and we have a responsibility to the people of London to ensure we succeed.

198

Note

1. The views expressed in this paper are those of the writer and are not meant to represent the collective views of the Police Service.

Acknowledgments

This volume arose from a conference on drug couriers organized by the Howard League in 1991. Many thanks are due to all those who contributed papers to that conference and to those whose work has been subsequently incorporated into this volume.

Thank you to Alison Hamlin for her invaluable help with the manuscript. A very special thanks to Michael Grewcock at the Howard League for his exceptional patience, diligence and editorial expertise.

PG

About the Contributors

Rosemary Abernethy

Rosemary Abernethy is a probation officer with the Middlesex Probation Service Foreign Nationals Unit, England.

Hans-Jörg Albrecht

Hans-Jörg Albrecht is Professor of Criminal Law at Dresden University of Technology in Germany.

Nicholas Dorn

Nicholas Dorn is Development Director at the Institute for the Study of Drug Dependance, London.

Rudi Fortson

Rudi Fortson is a practising barrister, specializing in criminal law, in London. He has extensive experience of drugs law cases and has written widely on this and other areas of criminal law.

Penny Green

Dr. Penny Green is a Senior Lecturer in Law and Director of the Institute of Criminal Justice at the University of Southampton, England.

Nick Hammond

Nick Hammond is a probation officer with the Middlesex Probation Service Foreign Nationals Unit, England.

Olga Heaven

Olga Heaven is Director of Hibiscus in London.

John Hedge

John Hedge is Senior Probation Officer, Buckinghamshire Probation Service, England.

Tracy Huling

Tracy Huling is a criminal justice consultant working in the United States. From 1989 to 1993, she was Director of Public Policy for the Correctional Association of New York, Inc. and the Director of its Women in Jail and Prison Project.

Laurie Joshua

Laurie Joshua is Programme Officer with the Eastern European Division of Save the Children Fund. He was formerly the Policy and Training Adviser for the Fund's African Family Advisory Service.

John O'Connor

John O'Connor, now retired, was a Commander in the Metropolitan Police, London.

Rosa del Olmo

Rosa del Olmo is the Director of the Institute of Penal and Criminological Sciences at the Central University of Venezuela in Caracas.

Alison Stanley

Alison Stanley is a solicitor and partner specializing in immigration law at Bindman and Partners Solicitors in London. She was formerly a solicitor and caseworker at the Joint Council for the Welfare of Immigrants (JCWI) in London.

Ayesha Tarzi

Ayesha Tarzi is Foreign Offenders Co-ordinator, Inner London Probation Service.

Dennis Walton

Dennis Walton, now retired, is the former Head of the Drugs Policy Division, HM Customs and Excise.